EUL VERLAG

Reihe: Marketing und Kooperationen · Band 1

Herausgegeben von Noshokaty, Döring & Thun, Berlin

Angela Hund-Göschel

Music Sponsorship at a Turning Point

With a Preface by Tosson El Noshokaty

Bibliografische Information der Deutschen Nationalbibliothek

Die Deutsche Nationalbibliothek verzeichnet diese Publikation
in der Deutschen Nationalbibliografie; detaillierte bibliografische
Daten sind im Internet über <http://dnb.d-nb.de> abrufbar.

ISBN 978-3-89936-826-0
1. Auflage August 2009

© JOSEF EUL VERLAG GmbH, Lohmar – Köln, 2009
Alle Rechte vorbehalten

JOSEF EUL VERLAG GmbH
Brandsberg 6
53797 Lohmar
Tel.: 0 22 05 / 90 10 6-6
Fax: 0 22 05 / 90 10 6-88
E-Mail: info@eul-verlag.de
http://www.eul-verlag.de

**Bei der Herstellung unserer Bücher möchten wir die Umwelt schonen. Dieses
Buch ist daher auf säurefreiem, 100% chlorfrei gebleichtem, alterungsbestän-
digem Papier nach DIN 6738 gedruckt.**

Geleitwort der Herausgeber zur Veröffentlichungsreihe

Betriebswirtschaftliche (Fach-)Literatur steht immer im Spannungsfeld zwischen Theorie und Praxis: Einerseits ist eine wissenschaftliche Aufarbeitung von Themen unabdingbar, um Gegebenheiten und Zusammenhänge systematisch aufzudecken und somit gewonnene Erkenntnisse übertragbar sowie anwendbar zu machen. Andererseits muss das wissenschaftliche Vorgehen zwangsläufig seinen Ausgangspunkt bei den praktischen Herausforderungen des Unternehmensalltags nehmen, um nicht als „l'art pour l'art" ohne praktische Relevanz wahrgenommen zu werden.

Im Marketing wird der Brückenschlag zwischen Theorie und Praxis allerdings zusätzlich erschwert: Während auf wissenschaftlicher Seite klar zwischen „Marketing als marktorientierte Unternehmensführung" (d.h. einer ganzheitlichen Ausrichtung der Unternehmensführung am Markt) und „Marketing als eine Funktion der Unternehmensführung" unterschieden wird, werden die Begrifflichkeiten in der Praxis höchst uneinheitlich verwendet. Mal wird mit Marketing der eine, mal der andere Ansatz bezeichnet; in funktionaler Hinsicht wird der Begriff mal synonym (!) für kommunikative Aktivitäten wie z.B. Werbung und Öffentlichkeitsarbeit, mal für vertriebliche Aktivitäten eingesetzt. Häufig mangelt es sogar innerhalb ein und desselben Unternehmens an einem einheitlichen Verständnis, woraus sich im schlimmsten Fall eine Fehleinschätzung der Marketingeinheiten hinsichtlich ihres Gesamt-Wertbeitrags im Unternehmen ergibt. Vielleicht ist es auch auf dieses Missverständnis zurückzuführen, dass nicht wenige Praktiker dazu neigen, den Marketinggrundgedanken auf das eigene „abnehmerorientierte" Verhalten zu übertragen – mit der Folge, dass fortlaufend neue, scheinbar „besser zu verkaufende" Begrifflichkeiten geprägt und Themen als ‚next big thing' im Marketing angepriesen werden.

Unabhängig davon, ob dies zu Kritik von wissenschaftlicher Seite an Oberflächlichkeit/"Marketing-Blabla" und „Ver-Englischung" führt oder nicht – ein Diskurs über die wirklich relevanten Themen wird aus den oben genannten Gründen deutlich erschwert.

Mit der Schriftenreihe „Marketing und Kooperationen" möchten wir einen kleinen praktischen Beitrag für den Brückenschlag zwischen Theorie und Praxis leisten. In dieser Reihe werden ausgewählte deutsch- und englischsprachige Diplom-/Masterarbeiten veröffentlicht, die wir im Rahmen unserer Tätigkeit als Agentur für Marketing und Kooperationen betreut haben. Ausgangspunkt aller Arbeiten sind entsprechend konkrete Fragestellungen aus der Unternehmenspraxis, keine (potenziellen) „Hype-Themen".

Die Autoren bearbeiten diese Fragestellungen unter Berücksichtigung aktueller wissenschaftlicher Erkenntnisse, stellen Zusammenhänge zu anderen Themenfeldern her und/oder nehmen eine vergleichende Analyse unterschiedlicher Ansätze vor. In der Regel bildet eine Ableitung von Handlungsempfehlungen für die Praxis den Abschluss der Arbeiten.

Auftakt bildet die Ihnen vorliegende, englischsprachige Abschlussarbeit „Music sponsorship at a turning point", die sich mit den derzeitigen Veränderungen im Musikmarkt und den daraus resultierenden Chancen und Risiken für (potenzielle) Musiksponsoren beschäftigt.

Wir hoffen, mit der Veröffentlichung dieser Arbeiten und dem darin vollzogenen „doppelten Brückenschlag" von praktischen Aufgabenstellungen zu wissenschaftlicher Bearbeitung und zurück zu praxisnahen Leitlinien interessante Denkanstöße für Theorie und Praxis zu wirklich relevanten Marketingthemen geben zu können.

Berlin, Juli 2009

Tosson El Noshokaty, Jan Döring, Simon Thun

Geschäftsführende Gesellschafter, Noshokaty, Döring & Thun GmbH

Preface

"The times they are a-changin'" – the title of Bob Dylan's third studio album is regularly being borrowed when referring to continuous changes in business environments. Regarding sponsoring there is a double truth to this quote: Within a long-term perspective, sponsoring has evolved from the early days of (altruistic) patronage to an effective marketing instrument in current times. And in addition, looking at recent years, there have been significant shifts between the different sponsoring markets, especially between the sports market and the cultural market.

Within the area of the cultural market, the music market plays a dominant role. By part this is certainly due to the fact that music is a universal topic: In the same way that one cannot actively avoid listening, music is a topic almost everyone can relate to in one or another way (everyone has some sort of favourite music, but not everyone is a friend or active pursuer of sports, let alone visual arts). And where the people are, the marketers follow: Companies are increasingly making use of music in their marketing approach – with global top brands like Coca-Cola taking the lead.

The work at hand takes an in-depth look at sponsorship in the music market. Based on a definition and profound analysis of the market of sponsorships, its origin, characteristics different types and latest developments, the author analyses the market of music sponsorship in detail. As a structuring element Porter's "Five Forces" Model is being applied to the music industry, helping to gain a better understanding of the driving forces in the market – including a specification of the main potential sponsoring partners.

Besides a good overview of the music market in general and the market for music sponsorship in specific, the key result of the work at hand is an outline of opportunities and threats for sponsors in the music market. Hereon, the author provides strategic advice for companies considering sponsoring activities in the music market. This is most certainly as well of interest for companies considering other (co-operation) measures with and/or within the music market. Even if they do not have any experiences in the music market to date – it is never too late to consider. Or as Bob Dylan put it: "The slow one now – will later be fast – as the present now – will later be past".

Berlin, July 2009

Tosson El Noshokaty

Noshokaty, Döring & Thun

Acknowledgement

I would like to express my sincere appreciation to Simon Thun, co-founder of Noshokaty, Döring & Thun, for his inspiring contribution and excellent mentoring throughout the course of the thesis.

Berlin, July 2009
Angela Hund-Göschel

Index of Contents

Index of Figures

Index of Tables

Limits of the thesis and terms used

The focus of this bachelor thesis lies on the perspective of companies as potential sponsor and therefore leaves aside certain aspects of the sponsored party's point of view. Moreover, the thesis is written in an international scope and takes into account developments and trends on the global sponsoring and music market. However, as the thesis was written in Germany, also examples from the German music and sponsoring market will be used to exemplify global developments and trends.

The executed music industry analysis focuses on key developments with most impact on the market and confines to the respective key players that were affected most (i.e. record labels and artists/bands). The opportunities and threats deduced from these key developments have a selective and representative character, do not claim to be complete, and aim to illustrate the change in conditions for potential sponsors on the music market.

Moreover, information of reference texts in German was translated into English, which will not be specifically marked within the footnotes (except quotations). Furthermore, key figures of the markets will be given in the currency Dollar ($) when referring to international figures, and in Euro (€) in relation with figures from the German market.

The convention of the terms "sponsorship" and "sponsoring" differs within the German and English literature, and even within the English literature both terms are used variedly. In this regard, in the following the term sponsorship will be used exclusively as a noun, while the term sponsoring will always appear as an adjective (e.g. sponsoring markets).

Within the thesis the "music industry" is also referred to as "music market", "music sector" or "music business". For the purpose of this thesis, no further differentiation of these terms is necessary.

The term "360 degree activation" refers to the implementation of sponsoring measures throughout all marketing platforms and products.

The expression "360 degree deal" means an all-encompassing contract between an artist and a company that covers all issues related to the artist and its products, i.e. regarding recording, touring, merchandising and publishing.

The phrases "short-term", "mid-term" and "long-term" financial objectives were used to describe the sponsors' different economic expectations. Thereby, "short-term" means instantly (during the measure, e.g. sales at events), "mid-term" refers to few weeks after the sponsoring measures were implemented and "long-term" means months (up to years) after the measures were conducted.

At times, especially in the last chapter, most relevant points were marked **bold** in order to ease the screening for key information and to render additional figures/tables unnecessary.

1. Introduction

U2 has done it, Madonna has done it and so did Jay-Z, Shakira and Nickelback just a few weeks ago. One can read almost daily about another artist closing a "360 degree deal" with an event management organisation for the production and marketing of their music and image, i.e. signing one single, all-including contract instead of having a set of deals with record labels, managers, promoters etc. Presently, the whole music industry seems to be at a turning point, and this is one of the most visible implications. Thanks to technologies like the Internet and the digitalisation of music, numerous observable changes are taking place within the music industry.

These developments might also be of high interest for companies of other industries. The emotional product of music is generally gaining societal relevance and already offers various application opportunities for the achievement of the companies' image and marketing objectives. The inset of sponsorships has become a widely appreci-ated tool for image-, but also sales- and relationship-oriented purposes. However, companies worldwide still utilise sponsorships comparatively little on other markets than the sports market, which currently faces tremendous image problems. Due to the latest developments in society and advertising as well as changes and trends within the music industry itself, the music market might be on of the most promising market for sponsorships today.

The objective of this thesis is to show how companies can take advantage of the latest developments within the music industry for the purpose of sponsorship. Accordingly, it will be revealed which opportunities and threats the music industry provides to sponsors, particularly with regard to these latest developments. Concluding, the thesis will provide a strategic checklist for the planning of music sponsorships. The main question to be answered will be:

Which opportunities and threats does the music industry today provide for potential sponsors and what strategic aspects do companies need to consider in the planning of a music sponsorship?

In order to get there, following questions will be answered:

- What is **sponsorship**? What are the objectives of sponsors and how can companies achieve them by implementing different types and measures and on which markets?
- What are the specific, structural characteristics of the **music industry**, what key developments did it undergo within the last two decades and what are relevant implications for key players on the market as well as potential co-operation partners?
- How did the **market of music sponsorships** develop during the last years, what are key factors of success, applicable types and measures to be utilised?

Accordingly, the first chapter of this thesis provides a theoretic foundation on sponsorship, its definition, origin, characteristics as well as objectives and a deduction of objective-oriented types. The second chapter presents an analysis of the music industry along Porter's five forces as well as an illustration of the relation-ship between music and advertising market. Following, the chapter also incorporates latest developments within the market of music sponsorships, key factors of success as well as applicable types and measures. The third chapter introduces opportunities and threats for potential sponsors on the music market. This chapter provides a strategic checklist for companies with aspects of relevance for the planning of a successful music sponsorship.

2. Sponsorship

Sponsorships are mutual agreements, which companies increasingly often utilise for marketing and communication purposes. They were first implemented on the sports market, which is still the dominating industry. But due to image problems of the sports sector, e.g. regarding doping, and the more professional, selective and individual character of sponsorships, other markets could strengthen their position during the last years. This chapter will provide an introduction to the market of sponsorships, shortly portrait relevant key markets and illustrate latest developments and trends.

2.1 Introduction to the market of sponsorships

The mutuality of the sponsorship agreement, even if it is based on the company's will to support, is a key characteristic of sponsorship. It origins lead back about 50 years ago onto the sports sector, where they were mainly used for image purposes. Today, companies target very specific and diverse objectives with sponsorships, which make different types of sponsorship attractive for a rising number of companies, as can be seen within the latest developments on the market of sponsorships.

2.1.1 Definition

The term sponsorship is widely used nowadays and often laid-out broad. Sponsorships are often considered as altruistic forms of support like patronage or fundraising. Even though sponsorships are historically related to these forms of support, they need to be clearly distinguished. The key difference is that sponsoring relies on mutuality. The sponsor expects a reward for his support, which he most commonly utilises for communication purposes.

With growing importance of sponsorships during the last years, the variety of its definitions grew as well. The literature offers numerous definition approaches. One of the definitions that is widely accepted within the German literature was mapped out by Manfred Bruhn[1] in 1991:

---

[1] Bruhn, 2003, p. 5

Sponsorship means the

- planning, organisation, implementation and monitoring of all activities
- that are connected to the provision of money, goods, services and/or know-how by companies and institutions
- in order to support a person and/or organisation from the sports, cultural, social, environmental and/or media sector,
- and to simultaneously achieve aims of the corporate communication.

A second definition approach and one of the most compact definitions in international literature was established by the IEG[2] in 1982:

"A cash and/or in-kind fee paid to a property (typically sports, entertainment, non-profit event or organization) in return for access to the exploitable commercial potential associated with that property."[3]

Both definitions frame sponsorship as an agreement between a sponsor and a sponsored party with which both parties target specific, beneficial objectives. The sponsoring and sponsored party need to agree by contract about the specific efforts given by each party. Thus, the mutuality of the agreement is a key characteristic of sponsorship. But from the company's point of view this does not exclude the charitable motive of support. Many sponsors target to be recognised as supporter in the public rather than putting advertising motives to the fore of their sponsorship engagements. Volkswagen, for example, describes itself as "partner for music support"[4] and therewith communicates the image of a patron, although in the area of music they clearly functions as a sponsor.

---

[2] IEG is one of the globally leading consultancies in the field of sponsorship and part of the WPP Group, one of the world's leading communications services groups (http://www.sponsorship.com; http://www.wpp.com/)
[3] IEG Lexicon and Glossary http://www.sponsorship.com/Resources/IEG-Lexicon-and-Glossary.aspx
[4] Website of the VW Sound Foundation: http://www.soundfoundation.de/#/page/historie/

2.1.2 Origin

The idea of sponsorships originates in the altruistic patronage, a charitable support of groups and persons, and leads back to the middle ages. But as aforementioned, these patronages have nothing in common with sponsorships as they are defined today, behalf the underlying idea of supporting a person, group or organisation.

The origin of sponsorships as we know them today leads back 45 years to the American and British market. At that time, Gillette was one of the first sport sponsors entering a sponsorship of the one-day Cricket in England as early as 1963. Companies to follow were the beer brand Mackeson that sponsored the Cheltenham Gold Cup in 1968, and tobacco brands John Player and Gold Leaf. These are some landmarks in the history of sponsorships, but in reality it took a period of around 20 years for sponsorships to merge as a professional marketing instrument.

A good example for this slow but steady development is the Olympic Games. While the Rome 1960 Olympics involved 46 sponsor and suppliers providing everything from technical support to toothpaste the Tokyo 1964 Olympics were already sponsored by 250 partners, including cigarette brand Olympia, which generated $1million for the Organising Committee. For the Montreal 1976 Olympics, a total of 628 sponsors and suppliers generated $7 million for the International Olympic Committee (IOC) - not much by today's standards but a sign of things to come.

While sponsorships were solely implemented and increasingly professionalised in the sports sector in its first stage until the mid-eighties, companies soon also started engaging with parties from the cultural, social and environmental sector (see *Figure 1*). Ever since, sponsorships have professionalised in all markets and have developed into an inherent part of the communication mix of companies and brands worldwide, particularly in the economically strong North American, Asian and European markets. This also reflects in the growing importance of economic sponsoring objectives and a more extensive market structure, due to a growing number of market participants and continuously growing sponsoring budgets worldwide (to be illustrated within chapter *2.3 Latest developments and trends*). This again, implies an even higher necessity for individual companies to professionally prepare, establish and manage their sponsorships in a unique sponsoring mix in order to successfully differentiate themselves from other sponsoring companies.

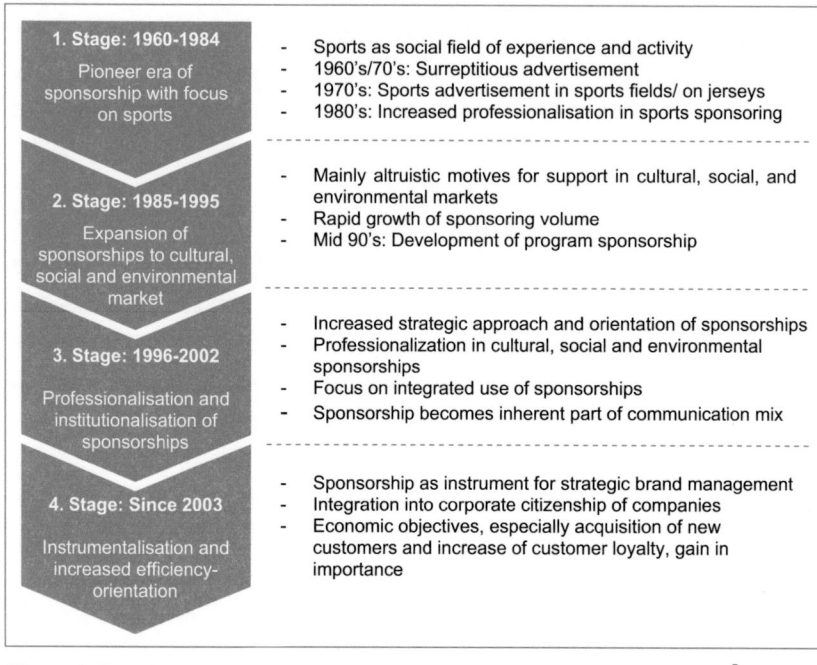

1. Stage: 1960-1984 Pioneer era of sponsorship with focus on sports	- Sports as social field of experience and activity - 1960's/70's: Surreptitious advertisement - 1970's: Sports advertisement in sports fields/ on jerseys - 1980's: Increased professionalisation in sports sponsoring
2. Stage: 1985-1995 Expansion of sponsorships to cultural, social and environmental market	- Mainly altruistic motives for support in cultural, social, and environmental markets - Rapid growth of sponsoring volume - Mid 90's: Development of program sponsorship
3. Stage: 1996-2002 Professionalisation and institutionalisation of sponsorships	- Increased strategic approach and orientation of sponsorships - Professionalization in cultural, social and environmental sponsorships - Focus on integrated use of sponsorships - Sponsorship becomes inherent part of communication mix
4. Stage: Since 2003 Instrumentalisation and increased efficiency-orientation	- Sponsorship as instrument for strategic brand management - Integration into corporate citizenship of companies - Economic objectives, especially acquisition of new customers and increase of customer loyalty, gain in importance

Figure 1: Development stages and milestones in the history of sponsorship[5]

2.1.3 Characteristics

As aforementioned, a key characteristic of sponsorships, in opposite to the altruistic patronage and fundraising from which sponsorships emanate, is the mutuality of the sponsorship agreement, i.e. the reciprocate exchange of benefits (e.g. in form of money, goods and services). In spite of this, sponsorships are often also based on the principle idea of a supporting a person, group or organisation. Another key characteristic is its communicative function of sponsorships. Sponsors and sponsored parties can engage in more than one sponsorship at the same time, but need to plan, implement and manage all of these sponsoring activities in an authentic and coherent long-term overall communication strategy. For this reason, sponsorships

---

[5] Hermanns, 2008, p.15 f

require a systematic planning and decision process. The joint communication and appearance within a sponsorship always generates an image transfer from sponsor to sponsored party and vice versa, even if not intended. A company or brand can utilise this characteristic of sponsorship for its benefit, by incorporating its sponsoring activities into its overall corporate communication policy.[6]

Key characteristic of sponsorships are:
- ✓ the principle of effort and reward,
- ✓ the idea of support,
- ✓ the communicative function,
- ✓ a systematic planning and decision process,
- ✓ the potential image transfer (even if not intended) and
- ✓ the affiliation to the company's communication.

2.1.4 Objectives and types

There are a various criteria to classify different sponsorships from the sponsor's and sponsored party's perspectives. From the point of view of the sponsored party the classification can be made according to e.g. the type of reward (commercial perform-ance, licensing etc.) provided, the own performance class (e.g. top-level or new-comer) or the type of sponsored organisation (association, foundations etc.). From the sponsors point of view a classification can be deduced e.g. from the type of sponsoring benefits (money, tangible means, services etc.), the number of sponsors (e.g. exclusive or co-sponsorship) or the initiator of the sponsorship (initiated by sponsor or sponsored party). But only many of these classification criteria can describe one sponsoring engagement at a time. A classification into types should therefore not only include the characteristics of a sponsorship, but also describe its strategic approach according to the company's overall communication objectives. Thus, a classification of sponsorships into types from the sponsors' point of view can best be defined in consideration of the sponsoring objectives.

---

[6] Bruhn, 2003, p.19 f

Previous to entering a sponsorship, both parties have to identify their individual objectives and need to evaluate whether these objectives can be reached by engaging in a sponsorship. Usually, the sponsored party primarily has financial objectives, but sometimes also demands goods, services and/or expertise of the sponsor. A company or brand as sponsor can pursue two basic objectives with sponsorships: Economic objectives (e.g. increase of turnover or sales volume) and psychological objectives (e.g. improvement of image or motivation of employees). About 90 percent of the German companies sponsor in order to reach objectives with regard to their image. Further key objectives are:[7]

- Relations to business partners and potential clients (86 percent)
- Increased company/brand awareness (85 percent)
- Relations to opinion leaders, media, etc. (75 percent)
- Customer loyalty (71 percent),
- Motivation of employees (69 percent) and
- Good citizenship (68 percent).

Only 34 percent of the companies name short-term economic objectives as one of their sponsoring objectives. The reason is that only companies that have a direct affinity to the respective sponsoring market (e.g. sports, culture), like breweries or soft drink producer as sponsors of music events, can utilise direct sales through sponsorships. In these cases, the sponsoring activities usually include sales promotions or personal sales. However, the named psychological objectives have a long-term impact on the company's image and can therewith be seen as an operationalisation of mid- and long-term financial objectives. It is already 62 percent of the companies, which target mid- and long-term financial objectives, and the importance of sponsorships, not only as a psychological, but also as an economic driver for companies is on a constant rise.

---

[7] Sponsor Visions 2007

A very clear and straightforward model to illustrate the marketing and communication objectives of a company is the Customer Relationship Path[8]. Sponsorships can address all five points (Awareness, Image, Consideration, Purchase and Loyalty) along the path and also offer the additional opportunity to activate relevant opinion leader and multiplier. These six points can be summarised in three strategic objectives to be reached with engaging in sponsorships: Raising awareness and profiling the image, activating potential and existing consumers and activating relevant multiplier. According to these objectives, three different types of sponsorship can be derived: Image-driven, sales-driven and relationship-driven sponsorships (see *Figure 2*).

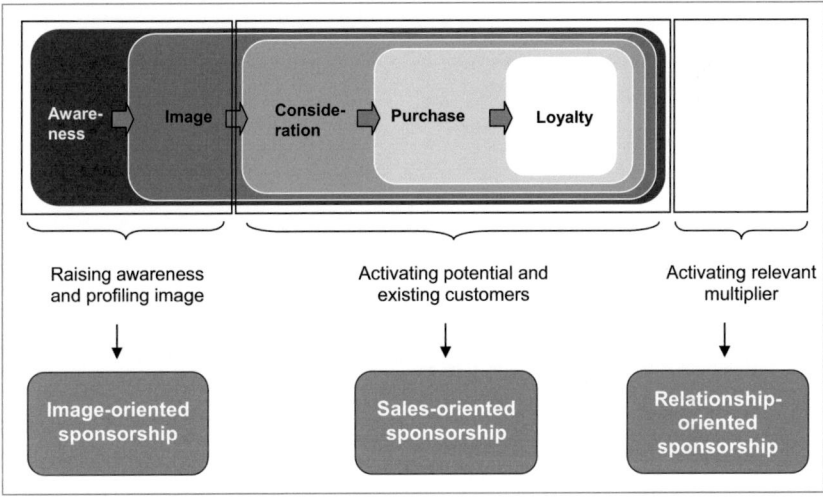

Figure 2: Types of Sponsorships deduced from the Customer Relationship Path

With the utilisation of sponsorships, companies primarily aim to raise awareness in the public. Consequently, sponsorship always implies a mutual image transfer between the sponsor and the sponsored party, even if not intended. That is why companies that are considering sponsorship always need to define their image-oriented objectives beforehand, i.e. decide on whether they want to raise awareness for the company or brand only within specific target group segments or the broad public. Furthermore, they have to decide on how to profile and emotionalise the

---

[8] Wirt, 2004, p.509

company or brand with the aid of specific image dimensions provided by the sponsored party (with regard to music sponsorship possible image dimensions will be illustrated under *3.2.2 Key factors of success*).

Marketing objectives along the Customer Relationship Path and deduced types of sponsorship[9]

Marketing objectives	Raising awareness and profiling image	Activating existing and potential clients	Activating relevant multiplier
Sub-objectives of the sponsoring company/brand	- Attracting public **interest** for the company/brand - Generating high **media coverage** - Creating and/or (re-) profiling a specific **image**	- Generating **purchase interest** - Generating **sales** - Increasing the frequency of **repurchases**	- Strengthening **media relations** - Strengthening the **relation with business associates** - Motivating its own **employees**
Exemplary measures to achieve the company's/ brand's objectives	- Logo Integration - Commercials - Press conferences - Product Placement	- Sales promotions - Product demonstrations and trials - Vouchers - Cross-selling - Sweepstakes	- Hospitality - Press releases - Free tickets
Type of sponsorship	Image-oriented sponsorship	Sales-oriented sponsorship	Relationship-oriented sponsorship

Table 1: Types of sponsorship according to marketing objectives

As aforementioned, more and more companies implement sponsorships for the purpose of short- to mid-term economic objectives (sales-oriented sponsorships) in order to activate specific target group segments of potential and existing customers. Furthermore they utilise sponsorships for relationship-oriented purposes, i.e. in order to activate opinion leaders, media and business associates (external) as well as their employees (internal). The classification into three sponsoring types according to the company's sponsoring objectives can help companies during the strategic planning process with regard the decision making about the broad variety of sponsoring measures (see *Table 1*).

---

[9] Own findings deduced from Wirt, 2004, Bruhn, 1991 & IEG Sponsorship Report 2007

Furthermore, a sponsorship can have different forms (sponsorship of person, group, organisation, event etc.) and be integrated into all communication and marketing measures (e.g. integration into classical communication, promotions, hospitality) of a company. The selection of a specific sponsorship is a strategic process of high complexity and all of the above - objectives, forms and measures - need to be taken into consideration. Another decisive condition for a successful sponsorship is the right choice of the sponsoring markets (sports, culture, public or media) within the sponsoring mix, because they offer different opportunities and threats to sponsors with regard to market structure, key factors of success, accessible target groups and image.

2.2   Sponsoring markets

From the economic and business point of view, sponsorship itself can be regarded as a market. The sponsor requires goods and services of the sponsored party and thus represents the demand side of the market. Accordingly, the sponsored party can be seen as supplier. The conjunction of supply and demand is the sponsoring market. The motivation to participate in this market is the achievement of communication objectives (sponsor) respectively funding (sponsored party). In principle, the market of sponsorships has a supply surplus, because many potential sponsoring projects meet limited sponsoring budgets. Further market participants are service providers, media and respective target groups. Service providers take in a connectional and advisory function. They can be involved in the conception, establishment and management of sponsorships. The media functions as communication channel and multiplier of the sponsorship by integrating the sponsors into their editorial media coverage. The target groups are the recipients of the sponsoring message and differ per company/brand respectively sponsored party.

Sponsorships can be utilised at four major markets: sports, cultural, public and media. Every market has its very own structure and key players with whom a potential sponsor has to do business. From the sponsors' point of view, every market provides a different environment and thus distinctive opportunities and threats. In order to give a basic overview of the four major markets, their respective key characteristics are illustrated compendiously in the following (see *Table 2 to Table 5*, p. 13 ff).

The sports market is the most popular sponsoring market. It provides the opportunities of broad reach, high media coverage and relatively high acceptance within the target group. However, sports sponsorships require relatively high capital in order to achieve broad reaches and are less suitable for addressing very specific target groups. Furthermore, there is a high risk of image damages to the sponsor, due to decreased performances or image scandals of the sponsored party. Cultural sponsorships are of increased interest for companies, due to a rising public interest in cultural activities. They can also provide attractive image dimensions and very specific target group segmentation. Nonetheless, they are less suitable for reaching mass audiences. Also, the sponsored parties demand a more sensible treatment than those from the sports market. Public sponsorship provides the opportunity of high public acceptance and national/international recognition and PR. It is a good instrument in order to demonstrate the Corporate Social Responsibility. In spite of this, the complexity of the projects and the dependency on political decision-making lower their attractiveness to sponsors. Media sponsorship is the youngest form of the four and offers a very broad reach for sponsors. Also, there are manifold implementation opportunities. At the same time, there is a high risk to be overlooked, as the number of sponsors expands rapidly.

Key characteristics of the four major sponsoring markets[10]

Sports	
Sub-markets	• Soccer • Handball • Equitation • Athletics • Golf • Cycling • Basketball • Formula One • …
Potentially sponsored parties	• Athletes • Sports clubs • Sports associations • …
Key Player in the industry	• Agents and Management of athletes • Sports associations and rights holder • Broadcaster and media • …
Opportunities	• Ability to reach broad, international target group during emotional leisure time moments • Broad acceptance by public when supporting youth work • High media coverage of specific sports • High reach during sportive peak performances during regional, national and international competitions • …
Threats	• Top-level sponsorships have high capital requirement, due to high competition in the sports sponsorship market • Athlete/team sponsoring bound to the risk of injuries or decreasing performance which leads to image loss • Limited sponsoring choices in top-level sponsorships due to high amount of sponsors (e.g. Michael Ballack had to lay off his sponsorship with Sony when becoming a player for Chelsea which's main sponsor is Samsung – a direct competitor of Sony) • …

---

[10] Own summary of research findings

Exemplary measures	• Tricot and advertising in sports fields • Classic advertisement (e.g. with a single athlete or team) • Sales promotion (e.g. autograph sessions) • Public relations (e.g. meeting with clients and business partners including prominent athletes) • Participation in events (e.g. VIP-marquee at tennis cups) • Use of title (e.g. official supplier) • …

Table 2: The sports market

Culture	
Sub-markets	• Visual arts • Performing arts • Music • Cinematic • …
Potentially sponsored parties	• Single persons or cultural groups • All kinds of organisations and associations • …
Key Player in the industry	• Musicians, artists • Cultural groups and associations • Manager, agents, record label, rights holders • Media • …
Opportunities	• Increased interest of the public in culture • High acceptance and attention within the public • Very specific target groups can be addressed • Increased interest of hardly accessible target group segments (e.g. youth, higher educated) • Attractive image values which can also be utilised for a company's Corporate Identity and internal communication • Regional or national broadcast • Good reputation within circles opinion leader and multiplier • The sponsor can distinguish himself more clearly and often appears exclusively (compared to sports) • …
Threats	• The sponsored party demands for a more sensible treatment than in sports sponsorships • Barely the chance to appropriately approach a mass audience • …

Exemplary measures	• Promotion of young talents and first exhibitions • Presence at events (theatre spectacle etc.) and exhibitions (museum, galleries of art) • World or art and work (e.g. exhibitions of companies) • Public Relations (Press releases) • Image advertising (programs, posters, advertisements) • Participation in events (VIP performances for selected clients) • ...

Table 3: The cultural market

Public	
Sub-markets	• Environment • Social • Science • ...
Potentially sponsored parties	• Organisations and associations • ...
Key Player in the industry	• Universities • Organisations from the health, environmental, animal rights, monument protection, self-help sector • Media • ...
Opportunities	• High realisation rate with complex projects • High public acceptance • National/International recognition and PR • Increasing number of memberships in initiatives and groups • ...
Threats	• Low stage of development • Connection of public areas with economic interests problematical (rather utilised with corporate giving") • Technical infrastructure is missing • Only few transport possibilities of high-capacity • Only small funds for advertisement • Dependency of the political decision-making • ...
Exemplary measures	• Image advertising (mention on devices, vehicles etc.) • Public Relations (press releases, image brochures) • Naming of the sponsor in all communication activities (media and member information, annual reports) • ...

Table 4: The public market

Media	
Potentially sponsored parties	• TV, Radio or Online Programs • TV, Radio or Online Networks • …
Key Player in the industry	• TV, Radio or Online Networks • Broadcaster • Agencies • …
Opportunities	• Broad reach within specific target groups • Manifold implementation possibilities • …
Threats	• Youngest form of sponsorship • High risk to be overlooked due to high number of sponsors • …
Exemplary measures	• Logo Placement • Trailer • Internet banner • Pop-ups • Product Placement • …

Table 5: The media market

2.3   Latest developments and trends

In its earliest days, sponsorship was almost exclusively the domain of sports properties. In 1984, 90 percent of all sponsorship dollars went to sports[11], and sport sponsorships continue to command the lion's share of the sponsoring budget. But the companies' demand of co-operations for a new and better way of communicating with their key audiences has benefited every type of sponsorship.

Nowadays, more and more companies use their sponsorship strategy to combine single advertising, public relations or sales promotion measures. The measures are integrated into the overall sponsorship strategy and therewith offer communication opportunities, which are quite different from all other marketing tools. Thus, sponsorships can be a highly efficient image carrier when closely linked to the integrated marketing and communication effort.

The growing significance of sponsorship is also reflected in its global budget. The IEG Sponsorship Report[12] forecasts a continuation of the ongoing trend on the sponsoring market. According to IEG, the 2008 global spending on sponsorship should reach $43.5 billion, a 14.8 percent increase over this year's $37.9 billion. European companies will raise sponsorship spending by 11.6 percent from $9.5 billion in '06 to $10.6 billion in 2008. Asia Pacific companies will hike budgets 15.6 percent from $6.4 billion to $7.4 billion, Central and South American companies will see an 11.1 percent jump from $2.7 billion to $3 billion; and companies based in all other regions will grow expenditures 5.9 percent from $1.7 billion to $1.8 billion. Spending on sponsorship by North American companies will grow at the brisk pace of 12.6 percent in 2008. It is the sixth consecutive year that the growth rate will be higher than the year before and the biggest jump since 2000, according to IEG Sponsoring Report's 23rd annual industry forecast.

As a key market of sponsorships, companies in Germany also increased their spending on sponsorship considerably during the last years. The 2006 World Cup in soccer hyped the so far steady growth. In 2007, sports sponsoring made €2.5 million

---

[11] IEG Sponsorship Report 2007
[12] IEG Sponsorship Report 2007

of the total of €4 million, while media sponsoring reached €0.9 million and cultural and public sponsoring each €0.3 million. According to the Sponsor Visions 2007, total spending is predicted to reach an all-time high of €4.4 million in 2009, even with no greater sporting event coming up. But in Germany the share of sports sponsoring also account for most sponsoring spending.

The most important trend within the market of sponsorship is the further profession-nalization of all conceptual and executive activities during the sponsoring process due to an increased business orientation, especially in the cultural and public markets. Personal preferences of decision makers on the sponsor's side still play a role with the selection of the sponsorship, but increasingly loose weight in the course of its professionalization.[13] Consequently, prospects on sponsorships grow and sponsoring funds are allocated to a small number of well-established sponsorships. This trend is likely to continue during the next years. Market participants will *professionalise* and sponsors *will focus on fewer, but more extensive sponsoring engagements*. The *understanding of sponsorships as strategic partnerships* will continue to grow and sponsored parties will start to increase their co-operation efforts for the development of *specific sponsorship solutions*.

---

[13] Bruhn, 2003, p.366

3. The market of music sponsorship

Within the area of cultural sponsorships, engagements with the music industry have become increasingly popular. Global industry leaders like Coca-Cola, McDonald's and Nokia embrace engagements with music artists, groups and organisations for years already. They have recognised the increasing importance of music as a marketing instrument, as it plays a role in everyone's life and at the same time makes a statement about one's personal taste and preferences. This chapter screens the music industry as well as the market of music sponsorships for key developments and trends. The deduction of opportunities and threats for sponsors on the music market will be based on the findings of this chapter.

3.1   The music industry 2.0

The music industry is a very dynamic market, due to its high significance for the global audience and increasing market participation of supply and demand, which is facilitated by the latest technological developments and new opportunities provided by the Internet. There have been significant changes within the industry as consequence to the ongoing digitalisation of music, which lead to new trends regarding the role of key players, new distribution channels and consumer behaviour. The following chapter aims to provide an introduction and analysis of the music industry, gives an insight into the developments within the "music industry 2.0", explains the ongoing paradigm shift within the market and its impact on the relation of music and advertising market.

3.1.1 Introduction to the music industry

The terms music industry relates to the business of music and describe - in a narrow sense – "all activities that are related to music businesses and organisations that record, produce, publish, distribute, and market recorded music"[14]. This corresponds to the International Standard Industrial Classification (ISIC) that includes sound recording and music publishing activities.[15] "In a broader sense, the industry also compasses a range of sub-industries including programming and broadcasting

---

[14] Definition on Wikipedia for "Music Industry" (May 2008), http://en.wikipedia.org/wiki/Music_industry
[15] The "International Standard Industrial Classification of All Economic Activities" is a United Nations system for classifying economic data

activities, information and communication, arts and entertainment, education and instrument manufacturer. In this broader sense, the term usually also encompasses not-for-profit organizations such as Musicians' Unions and writers' copyright collectives and performance rights organisations."[16]

The Status Quo of the music industry is the following: The recording and retail sector of the music industry suffer from a grave crisis ever since the digitalisation of music set in, after having a short-term boom due to the introduction of the Compact Disc in 1983. The recording market is primarily affected and struggles with a strong decline in sales, but is still representing the centrepiece of the whole industry. According to IFPI Germany, that pictures 86 percent of the German music market, total revenues of the industry declined by 42 percent from 1997 to 2005.[17]

3.1.2 The music industry along Porter's Competitive Forces Model

When evaluating the key components of the music industry many analysing tools can be utilised for the purpose of illustration and explanation. In this context, a proven remedy and a framework for industry analysis and business strategy development is the five forces model of Michael E. Porter.[18] It uses concepts developed in Industrial Organization (IO) economics to derive five forces that determine the competitive intensity and therefore attractiveness of a market. According to Porter, it is a condition to know and understand the "rules" of a specific industry in order to successfully select a strategy for the entry onto a market. In order to evaluate the attractiveness of the music market for potential sponsors later on in this thesis, it is meaningful to first examine the music industry itself.[19]

According to Porter, the structure of an industry is determined by five competitive strengths. Besides the competitive rivalry within an industry, it is the bargaining power of suppliers, the bargaining power of customers, the threat of new entrants and the threat of substitute products (also see *Figure 3*). The respective structure of each of the five forces determines, which companies are able to realise profitability

---

[16] Definition on Wikipedia for "Music Industry" (May 2008), http://en.wikipedia.org/wiki/Music_industry
[17] Spiesecke, 2005, p.11
[18] Porter, 1998, p. 7
[19] Porter, 1998, p. 26 ff

potentials on this market and to which extent. The bargaining power of supplier and customers, for example, has impact on price, turnover and costs, while the competitive rivalry is a decisive factor for equity requirements.

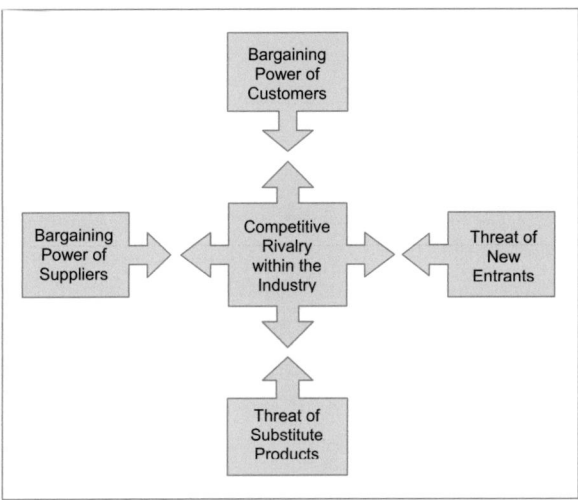

Figure 3: The five forces model according to Porter

Until the end of the last century, the processes within the global music industry were quite established and predictable: it consisted of the four major record labels Sony BMG, EMI, Universal and Warner, which had about 75 percent market share globally. Smaller suppliers, the so-called independent labels, and mid-sized record labels, the major independent labels, shared the other 25 percent of the market. But with a market share of three-fourths, it was the four majors, which basically held all the strings, i.e. the main rights in the music exploitation process. A lot has changed in the music industry in the last decade though. This also means that the competitive forces model for the industry has changed. In order to illustrate the drastic changes, both – the "old" and the "new" music industry – will be analysed according to Porter in the following.

3.1.2.1   The "old" music industry

Until the late 1990's the situation in the music industry was dominated by high demand (by artists) and very limited supply (of record deals by the labels). Usually, a newcomer artist went to a major record label or a larger independent and applied for a record deal. Chances were very low to get such a deal without good contacts to the business and even if the artist got a deal, the record label could set most of the rules. Very few artists, for instance, actually had intellectual property right on their own music. Instead, the record company held all main rights.

It was also in hands of the record company to decide on the strategy for the artist. The label set all aspects of the artist's public appearance: from marketing budgets to the frequency of performances, from CD release dates to format, packaging and distribution channels of the music. At that time, the Compact Disc usually was the only release format. In some European countries the record labels even had a great level of control over the price for which the resellers were going to sell the CD's to consumers, as the four majors co-operate for their pricing strategy. For the Competitive Forces Model, this situation frames the following picture:

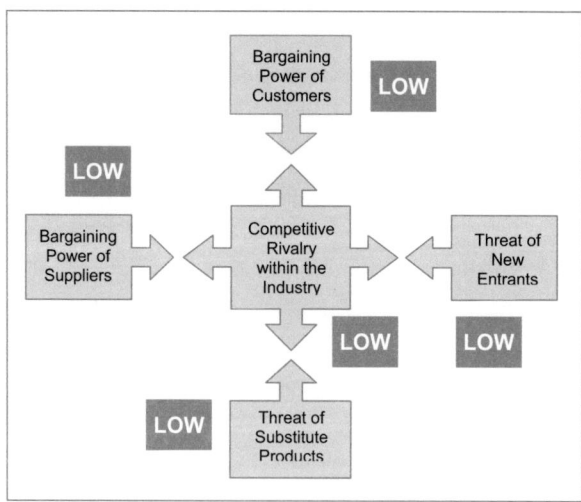

Figure 4: Porter's five forces applied for the music industry until the 1990's

Bargaining power of suppliers: low

The artists were very dependent on a contract with one of the "majors" or with an independent label in order to generate real success. Consequently, they only had little to say during the negotiations. In other words, a record contract for newcomer artists equalled a list of terms and conditions, which were universally applicable. This put the labels in a position of huge power and put the artists' bargaining power on a low level.

Bargaining power of buyers: low

For the consumers, the format in which they could buy the music and the channels through which the music was available were set. Additionally, the prices for which the music could be bought were controlled for large parts. So if a consumer did not like what he was offered, he practically had no way to get a specific artists' material through an alternative channel. Thus, the consumer were dependent on the products of the record companies, which lead to a market situation in which record companies could set nearly all of the rules and bargaining power of buyers was low.

Threat through new entrants: very low

Although there are numerous smaller independent record labels, entering the music industry with a new record label that was competitive to the four majors was almost impossible towards the end of the last century. Building up new successful artists as a profitable product requires high capital, know-how and an extensive network. A lot of assets are needed in order to finance required production, marketing and performance costs for artists. However, more importantly the record label needs to possession an extensive network on different fronts to successfully sell its products. They need to have contacts at major venues were your artists can perform as well as with major stores through which your music could be sold. All in all it was really difficult for a new player to get sufficient market share. Thus, the majors did not fear new entrants.

Threat of substitute products: very low

Before the digitalisation of music took place, there was almost no threat of substitute due to the fact that music was only available and playable on one format and could only be obtained through one channel: the record company, which held the rights to the music. If consumers liked an artist, the only source for its music was what its record company was releasing. Music events were a possibility to see the artist, but not to get hold of his music. Thus, the threat of substitute products was very low.

Rivalry among existing competitors: relatively low
Until the 90's of the last century, the competition between the four majors and larger independent labels was great. On the other hand, their relative positions and market shares were pretty stable and even more importantly, the total market was more than big enough to serve this number of players. This meant that, although competition between them was fierce, each of them could be pretty sure they would still be in the business over ten years. Thus, rivalry was relatively low.

The Competitive Forces Model applied for the music industry until the 1990s provides the picture of a market where few players held all strings. The five majors co-operated to set most of the market rules and successfully kept out new entrants. The power of the major record labels also had impact on negotiations with companies for other industries. All crucial marketing components like price, place, product and promotion of an artist were almost solely determined by one of these huge enterprises and their clear corporate standards regarding the administration of rights. This made the establishment of new strategic business and marketing concepts very difficult and did not benefit strategic partnerships like sponsorships.

Basically everyone expected this market situation would stay that way and nobody assumed a new technology could have such a fundamental impact on these competitive forces: the Internet.

3.1.2.2 The music industry today
At first, it was the quick development of new computer technologies that enabled the introduction of digital media writers for CD's. Consequently, consumers started to copy, burn and physically share music without loss of quality. At first, this was no major concern as there were barely distribution channels for copied CD's. But it was the subsequent expansion of two new technologies, which completely disarranged

the music industry in the last couple of years: the introduction and global spread of the media format MP3 and the Internet. Thanks to these technologies music copies could be hugely compressed without loss in quality and quickly distributed through a global network. With the introduction of Peer-to-Peer programs like Napster people could now easily obtain a near-perfect copy of a CD for free and record labels see their control slipping away. Accordingly, the Competitive Forces Model has changed:

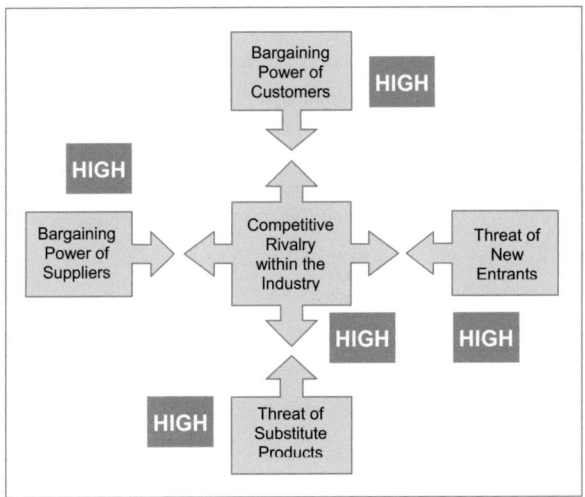

Figure 5: Porter's five forces applied for the music industry after 1990

Bargaining power of suppliers: higher

A lot has changed for new artists. Due to the Internet, they are less depended on the traditional networks of record companies and many started to directly market their material through their own website, social networks and music platforms. Many have even started to sell their own music through these channels, thereby completely by-passing the record company all together. Many established artists, on the other hand, have set up their own record labels and some have even started to distribute their music for free. This means they have acquired more control over their own product and that the record company has less control over the artist. Thus, the bargaining power of artists is higher, but they are still dependent on expertise and contacts of others in order to market their product efficiently.

Bargaining power of buyers: very high

The consumers of music today have more power regarding information and availability of music products than ever in history. They can now decide to download music for free, instead of being forced to pay a quit large amount for a CD in a traditional store. This means record companies have to offer their material for lower prices and through different channels. New suppliers have also begun to do so, e.g. Apple with its pioneer iTunes Music Store, which sold five billion songs since its introduction in 2003[20]. This development forces record companies to lower their prices and to listen to the wishes of consumers. In addition, it does not allow them to neither prescribe a music format to customers nor a channel anymore.

Threat of new entrants: higher

There are many new ways to enter the music industry through the production and promotion of artists. As aforementioned, it is now easier to set up an own record company for artists and others, because they are less dependent on the traditional sell-channels. Additionally, some of the new channels with a broad and established audience like social community MySpace offer new platforms of increasingly professional and popular nature to upcoming and established artists, which serve as a gratuitous stage for marketing purposes. Generating revenues with an artist today is a question of attention, which can for great parts be attracted for free in the Internet. Therewith, the entry barrier for new competitors is lower and the threat of new entrants like online services, virtual labels, Internet radio, private websites and social networks is increasingly high.

Threat of substitute products: extremely high

The threat of substitute products is now enormously high as consumers can download music illegally from the Internet, which caused a heavy profit collapse in the industry in the beginning of this century from which the industry never recovered. Record labels now try to cooperate with legal services, online shops and communities, but stepped in too late. As a result, there a billion of illegal downloads annually, causing a fundamental shift within the music industry's sources of revenue.

---

[20] Apple press release (19th June 2008), http://www.apple.com/pr/library/2008/06/19itunes.html

Rivalry among existing competitors: higher

As more players enter the market, the competition naturally becomes fiercer. The absence of creative ideas for substitutes to CD's and old distribution channels of the major record labels as reaction to the industry's rapid development has durably weakened their position in the market. They missed out on repositioning their core business to new sources of income. This did not only lead to decreasing profits[21], but to dissatisfaction of established artists, like Madonna, U2 and Jay-Z[22], who signed ground-breaking, all-encompassing contracts (including recorded music) with an event organiser instead of a record label. Additionally, online platforms that are co-operation partners of independent labels like eMusic constantly gain market share.

Today, the role of record companies is in constant development and it's not predictable whether substitutable institutions or organisations might take in their role in the future. The majors today are not only in competition with a rising number of new record labels, especially prominently owned ones, but practically with every source of music available to customers. This includes all legal and illegal music provider, online and offline. The major labels cannot take their market share for granted anymore and have to increase their differentiation to substitute products and rivals. Therefore, they have to reposition their core business, come up with new, innovative ideas and find partners for new marketing initiatives in order to tap new sources of revenue.

The music industry today is much more complex, faster developing and unpre-dictable than ever. The future role of record labels in the music industry is uncertain, but it is definite that they have suffered a great loss of power, because substitute products, bargaining power of customers and suppliers as well as the threat of new entrants has risen drastically. This development enables other industries to enter the market more easily and opens room for new ideas and sources of revenue also for them.

---

[21] From 2002-2006, the majors' revenues declined by 11 percent (Nielsen Sound Scan 2007)
[22] The Guardian (April 3rd 2008), http://music.guardian.co.uk/news/story/0,,2270696,00.html

3.1.3 The music industry 2.0 and its relation to the advertising market

For several years now there is a direct link between the music and the advertising market, which both underwent fundamental paradigm shifts within the last decades. The technical developments in the music industry have reached its first consumers a long time ago and affect practically everyone today. Due to the opportunities offered by MP3 and

> „The music industry 1.0 is over, one can even say it's dead. And every company believing it could make business as usual makes a fool of itself.“
>
> *Ted Cohen at the opening of Midem, January 2008*

Internet, music is literally available everywhere and for everyone by now. The one-way music industry 1.0 – as we know it – "is dead", according to Ted Cohen, former EMI vice president[23]. At this year's largest music fair, the Midem 2008, he took this statement even further and called up the necessity for an urgent reinvention of the music industry. But what recent news have heated up not only his, but the concern of the whole industry? And in how far do these developments have impact on the marketing of artists?

The amount of exceptional news from the music industry during the past year would be enough to give a full chapter for this statement. Artists like Radiohead, for example, became independent of record labels and started to exclusively release their albums in the Internet – thereby giving consumers the power to decide by them-selves which price they are willing to pay. Asked for the reason, Radiohead front man Thom Yorke stated at BBC Radio 4 that "the big infrastructure of the music business has not addressed the way artists communicate directly with their fans. In fact, they seem to basically get in the way. Not only do they get in the way, but they take all the cash."[24] Also other established artists like Madonna, U2, Jay-Z and lately also Shakira and Nickelback have cancelled their engagements with record labels only to sign all-encompassing contracts with event management organisation "Live Nation" instead. These artists have already started to participate in the marketing of their music, and even more important of their own person and image. And with the current loss of power of the record labels and renegotiated contracts that provide more rights

---

[23] Statement translated from original quote, Article on Börse Express (28.01.2008) "Die Musikindustrie 1.0 ist tot", www.boerse-express.com/pages/638529

[24] Article on Wired.com, 2007, "David Byrne and Thom Yorke on the Real Value of Music", http://www.wired.com/entertainment/music/magazine/16-01/ff_yorke?currentPage=all

to the artists, it is now also newcomers who start directing their own interests right from the beginning of their careers, also in order generate an authentic and sustainable image amongst their fans.

The main rights of the music exploitation, until now mainly held by the music labels and publishers, were focus of the economic utilisation until now. The trend heads for the economic use of marketing ancillary rights. Already today, the main share of revenues is not obtained with the sale of music itself, but with the marketing of its attending ancillary rights.[25] This development makes it appealing for artists, firstly, to increasingly market their image with less expenditure, and secondly to co-operate with the advertising market on their own initiatives (without record labels) in order to receive a greater share of their earnings.

A first consequence is a considerable change in attitude of the artists towards the advertising industry. While an artist was considered "buyable" by the public years ago, if he entered deals with the advertising industry, it is a common thing to do nowadays. The range of companies and brands co-operating with artists as well as the variety of advertised products and forms of these engagements has changed radically. While in 1968 Jim Morrison condemned the usage of his song "Light My Fire" in the commercial of car manufacturer Buick as a pact with the devil, it is today almost seen as a matter of course that an artist like Lenny Kravitz gets (financially) "inspired" by the values of vodka brand "Absolut" to exclusively write the song "Breathe" for the company. The subsequent campaign "Absolut Kravitz" was accompanied by a website offering exclusive downloads of the song's remixes.[26] Today, co-operations with brands have become an inherent part of the artist's image. So far, the prevalent and most important genre is still Pop music.

Equal to the music market, but not as dramatic, it's the advertising market that is transforming as well. One reason is the information overload consumers have to deal with; another one is the fact that consumers have become increasingly experienced with the marketing efforts of companies and brands. Today, our society deals more and more conscious, dependent on its own interests and also clarified with

---

[25] Ebenda, p. 342
[26] Also see www.absolutkravitz.com

advertising. And also here digitalisation comes into play. New technologies enable targeted recipients to ignore advertising message (e.g. through Pay-TV, advertising blocker, online video websites) respectively to selectively consume them.

Although classical advertisement and PR ("Above The Line") still marks up for the lion's share of the communication budgets, a trend towards non-classical advertisement ("Below The Line", e.g. sponsorships, product placement, sales promotions) has been noticeable for a couple of years already.[27] Also, advertisers have increasingly abolished the separation of the both advertising forms. Instead, they utilise various, single advertising measures as part of an integrated communication strategy, e.g. in form of music sponsorships.

3.2 Music sponsorship

In search of new modes of communication and a deepened dialogue with the target group, companies - especially those for which image and publicity existentially matters - have come back to supporting cultural groups and activities by means of sponsorships. During the last years, German sponsoring budgets for cultural sponsorships, including music sponsorships, have grown continuously and today they already are the second favoured sponsoring market besides sports (see *Figure 6*).

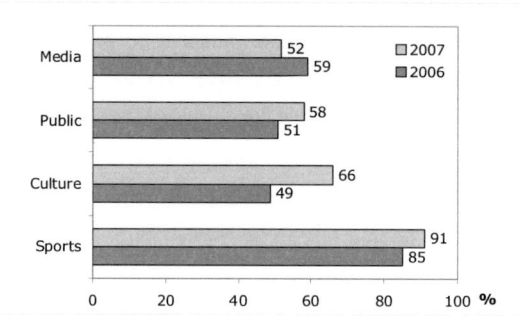

Figure 6: Development of sponsorship shares per market in Germany[28]

---

[27] Cp. Article on Clickz.com (23.01.2006), "Marketing spend shifting to Below-The-Line", http://www.clickz.com/3579096
[28] Sponsor Vision 2006/07

More and more companies like mobile operators detect the potential of music sponsorships and increasingly switch their sponsorship efforts from sports to music in the belief that it offers a better access to the youth market and better opportunities regarding the differentiation from competitors.[29] The result is an increasing relevance of music within the communication strategy of companies from all industries. Not least due to the fact that music sponsorships generally provide the opportunity for a strategic definition and stabilisation of the corporate culture and corporate identity on the long-term.

3.2.1 Latest developments

The market of music sponsorships developed very expansive during its early years. After exploiting its potential in the area of sports and its foreseeable saturation, the importance of cultural and therewith music sponsorships grew. Spending on music sponsorships in North America hit $867 million[30] in 2007 and is predicted to rise to $1.4 billion by 2011.[31] In Germany, companies invested more than €300 million in cultural sponsoring last year, of which more than 30 percent were devoted in music sponsoring[32]. About 38 percent of the German companies believe that cultural sponsorships will grow further in importance.[33]

Although the share of music sponsorships within the total spending on sponsorships is still relatively small, its attractiveness is continuously rising and it represents a potential growth market. A supportive factor for this development is the changing (ever more privately owned) media landscape in which sponsors have become a widely accepted institution. In the media today, sponsors are increasingly often presented in direct conjunction with the sponsored party, e.g. the beer commercial before a soccer game.

Another decisive factor for the rising importance of music sponsorships are the general changes within the structure of the society. During the last decades, the

---

[29] Spectrum Report 2006
[30] IEG Sponsorship Report 2007
[31] eMarketer 2007
[32] Sponsor Visions 2007
[33] Sponsoring Trends 2006

societies of most western cultures have developed an increased desire for cultural entertainment, especially music, due to the general development towards "leisure (time) societies" of these cultures. Enjoying one's life, individual freedom, singleness, unconventionality and the pursuit of pleasure are new cultural values and have been put ahead to old ones like family or belief. These changes in the societies' values had great impact on the consumer behaviour and leisure time activities. Additionally, other decisive factors have developed to the favour of leisure time activities, as can be seen in Germany. Average individual working hours are declining (from 1580 hours per year in 1995 to 1440 in 2005[34]) average disposable incomes (real) are growing (from €16600 in 1995 to €17800 in 2005[35]), and media consumption is on a peak (daily TV consumption in 2005 was 220 minutes, 59 minutes more than in 1995[36]). Summing up it can be said that the information overload and speed of present times arises the desire of many to know their culture and roots, and music has always been the absolute term in culture that is understood by everyone. Altogether, people, especially younger ones, listen to more music (and therewith create more stars in the music business) than ever before.

Today, music is a key component not only of Europe's cultural identity. The International Federation of Phonographic Industries (IFPI) describes the music business as one of the leading creative industries that increasingly drive the development of modern economies; and it is pioneering in the era of digital technologies and electronic commerce."[37] The music and entertainment market (broader music industry) was worth an estimated $1.4 trillion in 2007 and experts predict it will grow to $1.8 trillion by 2009.[38] The only sectors with decreasing turnover are the record company revenues and the music retail sector. Radio advertising revenues, instrument sales, portable digital players sales, publishing increased by an average of one billion in 2006 compared to 2005. The live music sector could even increase its revenues by $3 billion (see *Figure 7*).

---

[34] OECD 2006
[35] Destatis 2006
[36] ARD/ZDF Langzeitstudie Massenkommunikation 2006
[37] IFPI, http://www.ifpi.org/content/section_views/view014.html
[38] Pricewaterhouse Coopers, 2008

The music market - with its dynamic upward development in the past few years and the ongoing dislocation of sources of income for labels and artists - has great interest in this advancement of sponsorships. It opens room for ideas regarding new conceptual forms of sponsorships and offers new ways of showcasing them. Especially music sponsorships enjoy a very high acceptance within the public and are therefore often being showcased by the media. For companies, which sponsor artists, music events or programs it means that the public recognizes them as modern (48%), dynamic (34%), international (31%) and successful (34%).[39]

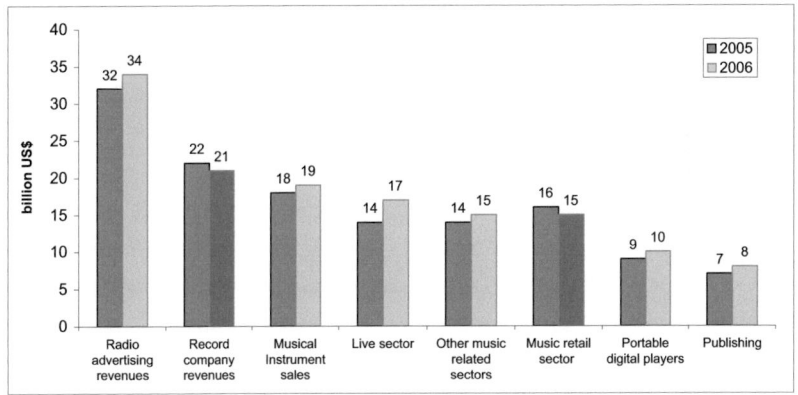

Figure 7: Turnover in the broader music industry[40]

3.2.2 Key factors of success

Music as artistic form of expression takes in an exceptional position within our culture, because music plays a role in everyone's life, even though with different intensity. Music is regarded as the language of all people and connects races and nations. Hans Heinrich Eggebrecht described the characteristics of music very accurately: Music features "the ability of expressing emotions... - Emotions in the sense of arousal, movement of mind and feelings, affect, temper, a physic and psychic state, which discloses by being abandoned... Therein, in its emotional nature, lies the exceptional position of music: it covers most directly within all arts the existential area of emotions. It can be only few notes, a sung or played melody, a

---

[39] German Survey on Sponsoring, 2006
[40] IFPI 2007

simple tune or an eccentric jazz song, from the theme of a symphony to the refrain of a Schlager to the leitmotiv of a movie. As a sounding emotion, music corresponds to the basic needs of people, of all people."[41]

Within the communication mix of companies, music plays an increasingly important role and is already an inherent part of the communication and marketing strategy of numerous companies. Music as a tool of expression takes an exceptional position in everyone's life. Due to its dependency on the music market, the market of music sponsorships is in constant development and so are the sponsoring objectives of companies. These objectives are basically similar to the ones to be achieved with other sponsorships, but the ubiquity of music in the society offers a quite unique amount and variety of opportunities to reach the sponsors target audience in non-commercial situations.

In order to successfully integrate music sponsorships into a company's communication strategy, potential sponsors have to take into consideration a number of key factors of success of this market. When planned and implemented advisedly, music sponsorship can benefit the embodiment of the company's corporate identity and be utilised in the whole scope of the marketing mix.

The key factors of success for a music sponsorship are[42]:
- ✓ the right choice of music genre,
- ✓ a careful selection of the performance class and
- ✓ reach of the sponsored party,
- ✓ the accurate approach of the right target groups (high target group affinity),
- ✓ a suitable image that a company wants to be related to (company/brand affinity) and
- ✓ credibility of the engagement.

---

[41] Eggebrecht, 1986, p. 5
[42] Deduced from Kohlenberg, 1994, p. 5 ff

The right choice of the music genre

For positioning a company of a brand product in an emotional landscape, the inset of music sponsorships can be an effective measure. But the range of music is eclectic and extensive. The following selection of musical genres can serve as a guideline for music areas, in which sponsoring can be applied: Classical and Contemporary music, Opera, Operetta, Musical and Ballet music (music theatre); Jazz; Pop and Rock music; Schlager; Folk Music, Electronic music and others (Chanson, vocal and church music, experimental music etc.).[43]

The displayed selection discounts the considerably more complicated reality of music types and interests. Yet the term Pop and Rock music itself implies various different music types and subgenres. In its daily use, the term Pop music refers to Popular, danceable music, including genres like Dance, Hip Hop, Rap and others. Rock music implicates genres like Rock'n'Roll, and Soft Rock, but also Heavy Metal and Punk to the point of Grunge and many diverse music styles with very different facets. Due to fluid boundaries between the concept of Pop and Rock music, both terms are going to be merged in the following. However, it must be pointed out that in part certain subgenres of Pop and Rock music are embossed by different lifestyles. Also in the case of electronic music, for instance, depending on whether its Minimal/Hardcore or Chill Out/Lounge music one listens to, there underlie significant differences in the philosophy of life within each grouping.

The public interest is different music genres is alterable and differs in every culture group. High TV viewing figures, for example, do not necessarily give information on Popularity, CD sales or music event attendance of a certain genre. For instance in Germany, Schlager and folk music shows have high viewing levels, due to the demographic development within the country, but turnover in the music industry are mainly generated with Pop and Rock music (see *Figure 8*).

Furthermore, the public interest in certain genres does not tell which specific artists, bands or events are favoured, but it is obvious and logic that a sponsorship only can be efficient if at least parts of the public prefer the artist, band or event or show

---

[43] Kohlenberg, 1994, p. 7

interest in the respective products and/or performances. The interest in an artist or band generally increases with his performance level, which is the second key factor of success.

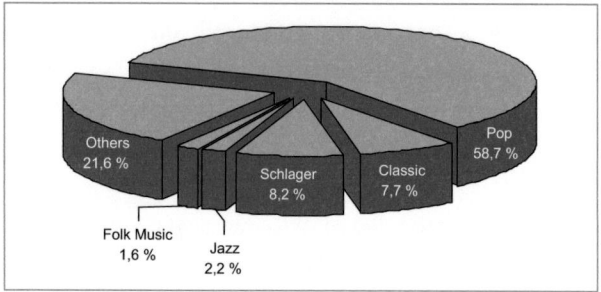

Figure 8: Revenue share of music genres in on the German music market 2007[44]

Selection of the performance class of the sponsored party

Music sponsorships can basically be applied in three different performance classes. The classification of the artists takes place according to the respective musical abilities and/or the prominence of the artist (see *Figure 9*).[45] To the lowest level, which can be called broad level, belong Non-professionals, for whom making music is a pure recreational activity. On this level starts the pre-selection of new talents. As a result of measures for the promotion of young talents, like the initiation of competitions, artists from this level are professionalizing. The second level, the performance level, includes artists who are accepted by the broad public, e.g. in terms of regular public performances. However, their prominence within the public can generally be regarded as low percentaged. The upper level, the top-level, consists of top-professionals, who generate outstanding performances and have a high market value. This group implies mega stars with a high degree of prominence and a national to global target group reach.

Accordingly, an idea for the potential impact of the respective sponsorship and necessary financial spending can be deduced from these classification criteria for music artists. Thus, the potential impact of the sponsorship will rise with an increased professionalism and prominence of the artist. At the same time attention should be

[44] GfK Panel Service
[45] Bruhn 1991, p. 42 and Hanrieder 1989, p. 129 f

paid to the fact that – in the course of the sponsorship – top-level artists are often defined as role models, which are alterable on short or long-term.

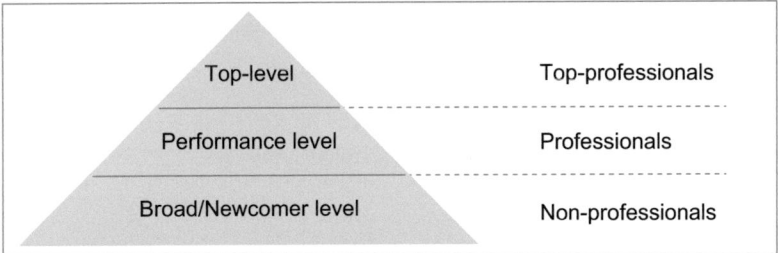

Top-level	Top-professionals
Performance level	Professionals
Broad/Newcomer level	Non-professionals

Figure 9: Overview of performance classes of artists[46]

It's particularly artists from the Pop and Rock music scene, who underlie the mechanism of short-term inconsistencies. The number of so-called "one-hit wonders" – which seem lucrative at first but do not catch the connection to their first success – in this area of music is on a constant rise. Potential investors need to develop a flair regarding this issue. Also some renowned artists from the Pop and Rock section have turned out to be unpredictable. The Volkswagen Sound Foundation[47], for example, has gathered negative experiences with top star Barbara Streisand in 2007. While Volkswagen was co-financing her first performance in Germany, the singer mainly caused a stir due to her exorbitant ticket prices of up to € 557 per ticket. Certainly, excessive ticket prices are nothing a business wants to be linked with. And even former "rebels" like the Rolling Stones, allegedly received four million dollars for giving a concert to an exclusive circle of 700 customers of Deutsche Bank, for which neither caused good press for Deutsche Bank nor for the Rolling Stones.[48]

Both "extremes", broad-level/newcomer and top-level sponsorships, have their advantages and disadvantages and should be selected carefully an in accordance to the companies overall marketing objectives and strategy (see *Figure 10*). While sponsoring newcomers mainly activates trendsetter and opinion leader and demonstrates goodwill within a smaller but more precisely definable target group, top-level

---

[46] Kohlenberg, 1994, p. 9
[47] Volkswagen Sound Foundation, http://www.soundfoundation.de
[48] Spiegel Online (27.08.2007), http://www.spiegel.de/kultur/kulturspiegel/0,1518,502216,00.html

sponsorships have a much higher reach and recall, as well as more publicity and a higher recall within the target group and media. With regard to top-level sponsorships, disadvantages are for example a higher liability to scandals of well-known artists, higher costs and increased competition with other sponsors. Newcomer sponsorships in turn have a far lower reach, generate less publicity and are confronted with a more critical audience.

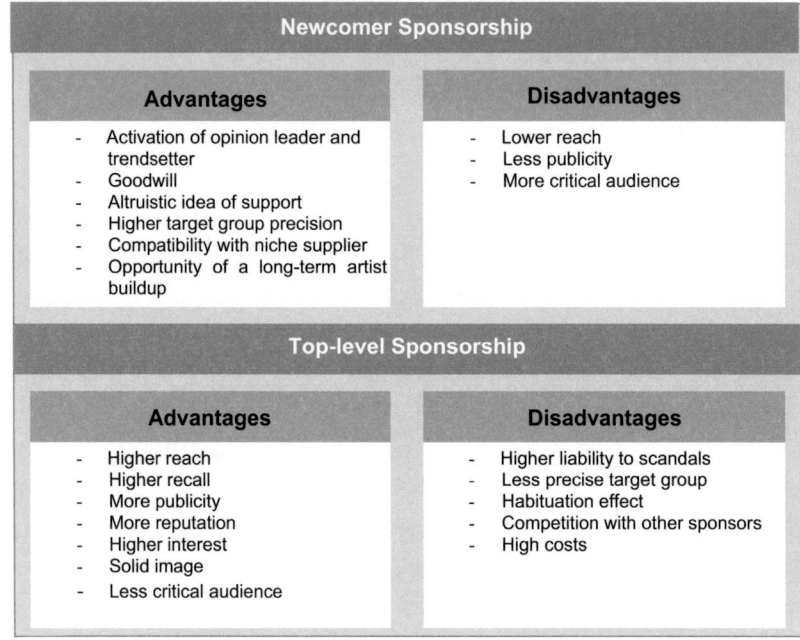

Figure 10: (Dis-)Advantages of newcomer and top-level sponsorships[49]

The logical conclusion is thus that the performance class of an artist also determines his target group reach, which is particularly interesting to potential sponsors and thorewith another important factor of success for the conception of potential music sponsorships.

---

[49] Jahrbuch Sponsoring 2008

Reach of the music sponsorship

The reach of music sponsorships in terms of media penetration can be defined according to the number respectively the share of people, which comes in contact with the sponsoring message one or more times.[50] Music sponsorships can be part of a globally or internationally oriented communication strategy, but also be implemented as a tailored concept for a national, regional or local market. Generally, the choice of the performance class of the sponsored party also determines the framework for the reach of the sponsorship. It can be expected that sponsoring measures with a high profile artist also generate a lot of attention, opposite to measures with locally known artists. If sponsoring artists from the performance level, potential sponsors need to consider that the degree of prominence and popularity might be high on a regional level but low on the national level, which leads to a lower the reach. At the same time, these sponsorships provide a high value added for the local community and can serve as a high quality communication tool, e.g. for local businesses.

An international-oriented music sponsorship with a top-professional provides the opportunity to position a company or brand within an internationally valid world of experience, as well as to overcome cultural and linguistic differences. With regard to the ongoing, global developments like the approach of the markets, the spread of communication and exchange media like mobile phones and the Internet and the new opportunities they offer for advertising purposes, international music sponsorships are increasingly feasible and attractive. Not at least because the international convergence unites new, little and until now less attractive, national segments to global respectively EU-wide target groups of economic interest.

Target group of the sponsored party

The target group planning is one more key factor of success for a successful development of a music sponsorship strategy. In order to avoid wastage, there should be a preferably high affinity of the target group of sponsoring and sponsored party.[51] A company usually knows its target group (potential and present customers,

---

[50] Nieschlag/Dichtl/Hörschgen, 1991, p.530
[51] Bruhn, 1989, p.19

opinion leader, employees etc.) regarding demographic, psychographic, geographic and behavioural characteristics, thanks to means of permanent data collection and market research. A segmentation of the target groups of potential sponsored party's needs to be deduced from the same criteria and should provide a preferably high fit with the target group of the sponsor, which makes a target group fit analysis as part of the strategic planning of a music sponsorships inevitable.

A suitable image that a company wants to be related to

As sponsorships primarily serve the purpose of a positive image transfer, a high image fit between sponsor and sponsored party is inevitable. The image dimensions of the sponsored party depend on multiple factors. Every individual music genre, musician, event, organisation and program has certain image values it is related to. The music genre is the most decisive factor, as every artists', events' and organisations' image depends on the kind of music they are involved in. For this reason, it is meaningful for the company to determine a small number of suitable music genres, before investigating on specific, potential partners.

With regard to cultural sponsorships in general, the most important image dimensions a company/brand wants to achieve with its sponsorship are: Competency, responsibility, prestige, and exclusiveness. Music in particular also has certain image values it is related to like innovation, dynamics, creativity, youthfulness, modernity, tradition, continuity, and harmony. Although there is no empirical data available for the image dimensions of specific music genres (those named above are speculative), this classification can serve potential sponsors as a first guidepost to a suitable music genre.[52] *Figure 11* shows an exemplary evaluation of these image dimensions in relation to the different music genres. With regard to the evaluation it becomes apparent, for instance, that it generally makes more sense for a financial service provider to sponsor a party from the classical music genre than one from the Pop music genre, as they aim to be recognised as competent and responsible.

However, finding the partner with the highest possible fit can only be achieved by evaluating each potential partner and his individual image values in comparison with

---

[52] Kohlenberg, 1994, p.34

the sponsor's own image objectives that he was to achieve within the broad public or specific target group segments. The financial service provider, for example, might also want utilise music sponsorship with a party from the Pop music genre for the purpose of creating a particularly young and dynamic image within the younger target group segment (e.g. with regard to the marketing of a youth account). In most cases, the information needed for the image fit analysis can be provided by the potentially sponsored party, as it knows its reputation and image within the target group and audience best.

Music genre / Image dimension	Competency	Responsibility	Prestige	Exclusiveness	Innovation	Dynamics	Creativity	Youthfulness	Modernity	Tradition	Continuity	Harmony
Classical music	X	X	X	X						X	X	X
Contemporary music	X	X		X		X						
Opera	X	X	X	X						X	X	X
Operetta	X	X								X	X	X
Ballet	X		X	X		X				X	X	X
Musical		X		X	X	X		X				X
Jazz	X			X	X	X						
Pop and Rock				X	X	X	X	X				
Schlager										X	X	
Folk music										X	X	X
Electronic music				X	X	X	X	X				

Figure 11: Evaluation of music genres regarding their image dimensions[53]

Credibility of the engagement

The credibility of a sponsoring engagement is a very important condition for a successful music sponsorship. If the target group perceives the co-operation between sponsor and sponsored artist, group, event, etc. as unauthentic, it may cause refusal within the target group (therewith lowering of sponsoring impact) or even cause damages to the image of sponsor and sponsored party.

---

[53] Based on Kohlenberg, 1994, p. 17

Many successful sponsors with high marketing/sponsoring budgets create a high awareness and achieve high reach with their music sponsorships. However, many of them also suffer from a lower credibility, due to the "perfect impression" they leave as a sponsor. With regard to music sponsorships, it becomes more and more important for sponsors to enter authentic engagements of high interest for the target group rather than, for instance, sponsoring global top-level artists with huge marketing budgets.

In general, the public perceives newcomer sponsorships as more authentic than top-level sponsorships, because these artists depend more on the sponsoring funds and marketing efforts of sponsoring companies. Additionally, the credible perception increases with the length of a sponsorship and with the artists' affinity to the company or brand. Thus, credibility is a key issue for music artists and a music sponsorship can only be authentic if the products and values of the brand/company are consistent with the emitted image of sponsored party.

3.2.3 Types and measures

A fundamental task during the conception of a sponsorship is to apply an ideal vertical coordination of the different activities that are linked to the engagement.[54] Hereby, companies can choose between numerous music sponsoring types and measures, which should correspond to the relevant target groups. Possibilities range from sponsoring music events to sponsoring artists or bands, music-related organisations, music contests and productions as well as sponsoring Online, TV and radio programs (see *Figure 12*).

With regard to the sponsorship of music events, companies can choose between the sponsorship of single events (in form of name sponsorship, presenting, title or co-sponsorships), tour sponsorships and own music events. The measurements used by sponsors in line with music event sponsorships depend on the music genre and intensity of the sponsorship. Exemplary measures are: Presentation of the sponsor's logo (e.g. on tickets, posters, tour busses), insertion in programs and brochures,

---

[54] Bruhn, 1991, p.407

press conferences, pre-promotions, product demonstrations and trials, hospitality initiatives and media partnerships with TV, radio and/or print media.

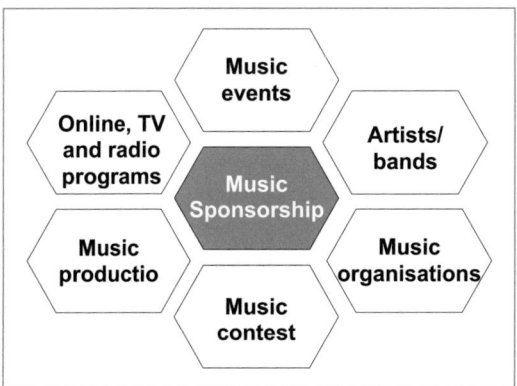

Figure 12: Potential application areas of music sponsorships[55]

The sponsorship of artists and bands means a co-operation with the respective party, which goes beyond the time frame of an event or tour. Besides the measurements named above, artist/band sponsorships can also imply additional measurements of support, like facilitating music productions or book publications portraying the sponsored party or integrating his/their performance in corporate and PR events of the company. The sponsorship of artists and bands provides manifold opportunities for sponsors when implanted on long-term. Sponsored parties from the broad/newcomer level might, for example, manage a breakthrough to the next performance level, and thus also increase their reach, thanks to the sponsor's aid. For the sponsor, this favourable development would provide the opportunity to generate increasing benefits by relatively small money. On the other hand, there is the risk of no or low performance increase and therewith dangers of an undesirably long contract period with little rewards for the sponsor. Supporting top-level artists does usually not involve the risk of low reach, but usually requires relatively high capital and also implies the risk of changing personality/image attributes on long-term.

---

[55] Kohlenberg, 1994, p. 48 ff

Typical music-related organisations to be sponsored are music schools and academies, music libraries, festival and opera houses, philharmonics, concert halls, clubs and live-music bars.[56] The support of these localities is usually limited to a local, regional or national scope and less experience less media coverage as e.g. the sponsorship of artists. On the other hand, these sponsorships are reaching a very accurately definable target group at places of their undivided interest, which makes it easier for sponsors to convey their sponsoring message to the target audience. Typical measures are logo and name integration of the sponsor, as well as joint marketing efforts for the venue and product presentation and trials at the locality.

For the support of a high number of newcomer or to-level artists, the sponsorship of music contests is a good opportunity. This can either be realised in form of an own contest (as part of an own music event or newcomer program, e.g. the 'Bit Music Contest' of beer brand Bitburger or the 'Volkswagen Sound Foundation'), or in co-operation with the organisations responsible for the arrangement of music contests, which differ per respective geographic market. In Germany, it is 'Deutscher Musikrat' (German umbrella organisation for music), public television networks like ARD and others, which mainly organise contests for artists from classical, folk music, jazz and popular music genres. When choosing between competing music contests, a company needs to consider its music genre and performance class as well as its potential reach, which is determined by the participants' proficiency level. The sponsored benefits might be monetary or in tangible means, e.g. financing produc-tions and tours or providing equipment such as instruments.

Due to a limited diversity of public music contests, companies have increasingly started to launch their own music contests and programs in order to directly address younger targets groups with the aid of music genres like Hip Hop and Rock. To establish an own music contest requires much more time, capital and communication efforts than a foreign-initiated contest. But once established, it can be the platform for a whole set of attention-grabbing marketing and communication measures. Beer brand Bitburger, for example, offers a complete package for the career kick-off of the winning band, including a MySpace presence, a photo shooting, booking and promo-

---

[56] Kohlenberg, 1994, p.63

tion of an own tour and provision of instruments, in co-operation with a manufacturer of musical instruments.[57]

The sponsorship of music production relates to the financial support of CD, LP, music video and digital productions. This kind of sponsorship is usually implemented in line with another music sponsorships, e.g. the one of an artist or music contest, like the 'Summer Sound' CD with tracks from newcomers supported by Volkswagen Sound Foundation. Another mean is the sponsorship of CD productions (usually contemporary or classical music) or sponsoring music compilations as well as music videos. The latter is not as common, but offers the opportunity to utilise product placements.

The sponsorship of music related TV and radio content is a proven remedy for many companies, thanks to its relatively high reach. Usually it is realised by means of title sponsorship ('Official sponsor' is shown at the beginning and end of the program as well as during advertising breaks) or in form of own co-produced programs, e.g. Coke brand Dr Pepper produced a show called "Dr Pepper Band in a Bubble" in co-operation with MTV and in line with its sponsorship of U.S. band "Cartel".[58]

These quite innovative concepts of sponsors, however, almost have to be considered as old-fashioned compared to the opportunities provided to potential sponsors by the spectacularly risen number of online music programs. To name only one example, it has been computer technology manufacturer Intel that enabled bands to integrate a music player for their own music productions into their MySpace profile, in co-operation with the new MySpace division "MySpace Music".[59] Today, each of the more than eight million bands on MySpace has such a music player.[60] Intel therewith provided the most popular MySpace offer in 2007 and an added value for consumers worldwide. Intel evaluated its initiative as a priceless, unexampled attention getter for the company's image.

---

[57] Bitburger Press Release, 2008, http://www.presseportal.de/pm/43064/1104800/bitburger/
[58] Dr Pepper Band in Bubble microsite, 2008, http://www.drpepperbubble.com/
[59] Intel press release, 2007, http://www.intel.com/cd/corporate/pressroom/emea/deu/
    archive/2007/372598.htm
[60] MySpace News Site, January 2008, http://www.all4myspace.com/news/

3.3 Learning

The present development in the music industry itself favours the prospects of music sponsorships. The Introduction of Internet and MP3 have caused a paradigm shift in the music industry. The long-established major record labels, heart of the music industry, are confronted with constantly declining turnovers, new and illegal ways of music distribution, and the slow but steady expiration of the CD as their principal source of income. As the labels search for strategies to stay competitive and music artists increasingly gain power regarding the marketing of their ancillary rights, companies from other industries now have the opportunity to co-operate even closer with them in line with more eclectic and innovative music sponsorship concept.

The developments within the advertising market and media, as well as the changes within the society are also advancing music sponsorships. Thanks to new technologies and an increased public interest and high media coverage of music events, music sponsorships gain an ever-bigger reach and create new opportunities to communicate with the target group. When taking into consideration all key factors of success, music sponsorships can provide a long-term contribution to the embodiment of the corporate identity for a rising number of companies and to the fulfilment of their communication and marketing objectives on regional, national or global level.

The following chapter will provide relevant opportunities and threats for sponsors on the music market arising from latest key developments and trends.

4. Opportunities and threats for sponsors on the music market

This chapter of the thesis provides a selection of opportunities and threats for sponsors in the music market and a short summary on what to consider before entering the music market as a sponsor. The first part introduces general opportunities and threats for music sponsors, while the second part deduces additional ones from four key developments in the music market. In direct assistance to this chapter, an elaborative checklist on what to consider before entering the music market as a sponsor is provided in the third part of this chapter.

4.1 General opportunities and threats

One of the most important opportunities that music sponsorships generally offer to companies is to **reach their individual target groups better than with classical advertising**, because it addresses people in direct conjunction with the emotional product of music. Also, the target group usually cannot escape its measures by, for instance, zapping as in TV or turning the page over as in magazines.

Additionally, the music market provides **very accurately definable target group segments**, due to fact that the music taste also implies general tendencies regarding brand and product preferences or at least for a certain lifestyle. These preferences can incipiently be deduced from stereotypes (e.g. a fan of alternative music is rather likely to buy from inexpensive no-name brands, while electronic music fans are more likely to buy premium brands and pop music fans rather prefer mainstream brands), but should then be supplemented with the aid of specific target group data collected by market researcher and/or the sponsored party. Thus, when selected thoroughly, music sponsorships can add a real value to companies for addressing specific target group segments.

For an effective reach of specific target group segments, music sponsorships provide almost **limitless opportunities regarding the variety of measures** to realise them. A company can integrate all of its marketing and communication instruments in order to achieve image-, sales- and/or relationship-oriented objectives with the sponsorship. According to these objectives and in line with the company's overall marketing and communication mix, the sponsor can choose between numerous measures like the integration of its logo and sponsoring messages, provision of product information and trials, the conduction of sales promotions, press conferences and hospitality measures.

Moreover, music sponsorships are an especially appropriate tool to clearly position and **strengthen specific image dimensions and values of a company or brand**. Due to the opportunity to address very specific target group segments in direct association with the emotional loaded product of music, music sponsorships generate potentially high image transfers between sponsor and sponsored party, which is as well an opportunity as it is a threat.

Potential sponsors also face a number of threats on the dynamic music market. In general, the scope of a certain music genre, event or artists/band is limited to a specific target group, which makes it **relatively hard to reach a broad mass audience** with music sponsorships compared to sports sponsorships for example.

In addition, the selection of the sponsored party is bound to certain threats. For instance, sponsorships on the broad and newcomer level require a long-term engagement in order to reach target groups not only on a local or regional level. As the **success of these artists/bands is not guaranteed**, the capital invested might not have the desired effect, to name only one aspect.

Another threat is a **potentially negative image transfer**, due to the wrong choice of the sponsored party. A low target group or image fit can quickly lead to a loss of credibility of the sponsorship within the target group and have strongly negative effects on both, sponsor and sponsored party. Music is a product strongly charged with emotions and music fans do perceive the usefulness of a music sponsorship very diverse. Hence, the multiplying effect of the product music with regard to image transfers in a sponsorship is a threat to potential sponsors just like it is an opportunity.

Also, it is crucial to implement all sponsoring activities in line with the overall marketing and communication policy as well as being aware that all sponsoring activities allow inferences about the corporate identity. By not taking this into account, the sponsor runs the risk of sending **contradictory messages and impressions** to the target group, which weaken the credibility and image of the company or brand.

4.2 Implications from key developments on the music market

In addition to those general opportunities and threats of music sponsorships, the latest developments in society, advertising and music market lead to new ones for potential sponsors. The three key developments in the industry are the general shift in profitable business areas in the music market, the drastic loss of power of the record labels and the resulting chance for other players of the music industry to produce and market themselves independently. Additionally, the Internet has become the key driver of the music industry. The implications of those key developments on the music market for sponsors in terms of opportunities and threats will be disclosed in the following.

Shift in profitable business areas: Live entertainment on a rise

Due to the increasing public interest in music, especially in live events, and thereby ascending media attention, companies and brands now have the opportunity to **sponsor also smaller events more prominently**, thus also with smaller funds. This makes music event sponsorship also attractive for smaller companies and brands. But also companies with greater marketing budgets can see their opportunities in music event sponsorship on a rise, as music live entertainment today represents an increased share of the broader music industry's turnover, reflecting the general trend towards concert visits. With the rising number of visitors, potential sponsors get to choose from a **strongly ascending number of diverse events**. Music events provide the chance to sponsors of presenting themselves within an environment charged with emotions within which the target group is much more receptive for the sponsoring message. Furthermore, the increasing amount of live events leads to a **higher number of eclectic integration possibilities** for the sponsor, i.e. a higher variety and quantity of measures to be placed during events or tours.

But this development also has as a consequence that more and more sponsors enter the music market. That makes the threat of **only being recognised as "one out of many"** very likely. Besides, the target groups get more sensible with regard to music sponsorship at live events, thus an **overload of advertising messages leads to a higher risk of negative image effects**. In order to avoid those threats, companies should only conduct a well-selected, differentiated set of music sponsorships and measures, which are exactly tailored to the needs of their specific target groups segments and implemented in accordance with their overall sponsoring objectives.

Loss of power of the record labels

The loss of power of the record labels has caused a great need for them to search for new business models. This gives the opportunity to companies and brands from all industries to establish relationships with the aim to **jointly develop new business plans**. On the other hand, the record labels have suffered a great revenue loss during the last years and therefore seek for the highest profit for themselves. This bears the **risk of conflicting interest** when it comes to co-operating with them. To avoid this threat, companies and brands should only approach record labels with a well-prepared set of ideas, wherein their own objectives are defined on a clear and measurable level.

Artists increasingly produce and market themselves

Regarding the sponsorship of artists and bands there is an evident trend towards a self-dependant management of production and marketing of ancillary rights, especially by established, top-level artists. This makes negotiations for a **co-operation with the musicians less complicated**, and thus more attractive to sponsors, due to the new absence of intermediary parties, like record labels. A new opportunity is to develop innovative **sponsoring concepts with 360 degree activation**.

One risk of those deals is the **lack of experience** of companies and brands with top-level artists. Also, up to now the **situation regarding legal aspects is quite unclear** in many cases, i.e. the necessity of involving third parties like management and record labels, for the marketing of the artists' music (main rights). Top-level artists are also becoming **more and more demanding and expensive**; they are thus not financially feasible for every company. Furthermore, an engagement with an established artist is increasingly often **perceived as exaggerated and pretentious**, due to their financial status, which actually renders a sponsorship unnecessary in the public perception. To avoid a negative impact on the company's image, the sponsorship therefore has to generate a real value added for the respective target group.

The Internet as key driver of the music industry

The new role of the Internet as key driver of the music industry is the most revolutionary development with regard to marketing. It provides a number of new opportunities also to sponsors. As artists increasingly market themselves on platforms like blogs, websites and social networking sites, potential sponsors have the **opportunity to detect and promote new talents and platforms**. Therewith, they can demonstrate their innovativeness, as so far only few sponsors make use of these platforms for their own purposes. Furthermore, the Internet offers various new ways to integrate and communicate the respective music sponsor. Even if it is not an online music sponsorship (e.g. of a online music platform), music sponsorships in general can now be **communicated with innovative and very eclectic online tools and applications**, such as microsites, branded blogs and social networking profiles. It also provides, it provides the opportunity for sponsors to **actively participate in the ongoing technological development** by developing new, branded applications and providing them – as a sponsored good and service – to online platforms and its users. A good example is the one of Intel and MySpace described in the previous chapter.

4.3 Strategic advice

The music industry 2.0 provides many innovative sponsoring opportunities for companies and brands. Nevertheless, companies should always establish music sponsorships on basis of a strategic planning in order to the threats. In the first step a company needs to **prepare itself for sponsorship in general**. The strategic approach of sponsorship requires goal-oriented marketing efforts by the company based on a detailed overall marketing concept. The concept should inform about corporate culture, image, customer needs, brand positioning, and unique selling points. It is furthermore important to determine the relevance of sponsorship for the company internally and to allocate employees who are exclusively responsible for sponsorships. Next, the company needs to set its overall sponsoring objectives.

Here, it is crucial to put the focus on image-oriented objectives rather than on short-term financial objectives. Although single sponsorship measures can also generate sales on short-term, the initial and overall objective of a company should be to position itself within certain image dimensions in the public perception. In preparation for sponsorship it is furthermore helpful to prepare and gain experience with events in order to realise preferably eclectic sponsoring measure. For measuring the effectiveness of its sponsorships, a company should also prepare evaluation tools for its sponsoring measures, like questionnaires for the target group or a database for comparing achieved media reaches.

The second key component in the strategic planning is the **right choice of a party from the music market**. Sponsorship as a form of co-operations implies the necessity to negotiate and interact with one's partner as direct as possible in order to avoid long communication channels, misunderstandings and phases of silence. Therefore, the company should look for a sponsored party it can co-operate preferably direct with and meet on a regular basis. When it comes to music sponsorship, the selection of specific and suitable image dimensions is a crucial aspect. The image depends on the kind of artist or organisation, on the related target group and the respective music genre. All of these aspects need to be evaluated in detail in order to ensure a high image fit of sponsor and sponsored party and therewith credibility of the engagement. Overall, companies need to analyse their individual situation in-depth and determine their individual sponsoring objectives and sponsoring strategy accordingly. Companies, which want to advertise on a regional level, for example, need to look for a partner that is known and popular within the region rather than a top-level artist. By supporting local acts, sponsors can win over the "public heart". By supporting national or international acts, the general public involvement might not be as high.

Thirdly, it is of greatest importance to **develop effective sponsoring measures** in order to differentiate the music sponsorship from those of other companies and to guarantee unique and lasting impressions within the target group. Key factors are the integration opportunity provided by the sponsored party. The sponsor should integrate his messages, services and products in an innovative way (e.g. acoustic and/or eye-catching), but thereby not detract the audience for the actual experience.

Music sponsorships can also be utilised for activating the media and other relevant multiplier (e.g. via information material or incentives). Overall, it is of great strategic importance to exploit the full potential of the partnership (e.g. though hospitality measures, corporate events, autograph session, co-operations with other sponsors) and to incorporate these activities with other marketing/communication measures (e.g. sales promotion, classical advertisements, public relations) as part of an integrated marketing strategy.

Thus, if strategically planned and implemented in line with all other marketing and communication activities, music sponsorship can provide a real added value for companies along all aspects of the Customer Relationship Path, activate relevant multiplier and even put the company or brand in a totally new perspective in the long run.

4.4 Strategic checklist for potential music sponsors

Step 1: Preparing the company for music sponsorship in general

- Does the company have a detailed overall **marketing concept**?
  The strategic approach of sponsorship requires goal-oriented marketing efforts by the company. The concept should inform about corporate culture, image, customer needs, brand positioning and unique selling points. These key principles of the company not only need to be set out in writing, but also to be communicated internally to all employees.

- Does the company believe in the **impact of (music) sponsorship**?
  A sponsoring company needs to be positive about the power of impact of sponsorships.

- Is the responsibility for sponsorships **settled decentral** within the company?
  Sponsorships are most successful if responsible employees can work individually and flexibly with regard to their time management. The daily tasks with regard to sponsorship should not lie with an executive employee.

·   Is the **board of executives** committed to the sponsoring engagement?
    In case of a decentralised management of sponsorship, the upper management
    needs to support those responsible for sponsorship internally.

·   Does the company have **experience with events**?
    Practically every sponsoring engagement includes an event. In order to conduct
    or participate successfully in events, it is helpful for the company to know how to
    arrange the event in a target group oriented and advertising effective way. If there
    is an event management subdivision in the company, it is meaningful to make a
    cross-link with the sponsoring subdivision.

·   Does the company **measure the success** of sponsorship?
    A company can only draw conclusion about the quality of its conception, by
    evaluating the outcome of the sponsorships. This can be done by questioning the
    audience of the sponsored party, executing interviews with other representatives
    of the target group or comparing the achieved media reach with those described
    within the sponsoring objectives. That way, the success of different engagements
    or measures can be compared over years and conclusions can be drawn from the
    observations.

·   Does the company set the **right objectives**?
    Sponsorships can accomplish a lot, but it should not be misapplied for the
    purpose of sales promotion. On-site promotions are an advisable measurement,
    but image objectives should always come before short-term economic objectives.
    Furthermore, the sponsoring concept needs to be deduced from the general
    marketing strategy and its public appearance needs to be in line with the corpo-
    rate design.

Step 2: The right choice of a sponsored party from the music industry

·   Is it possible to **co-operate directly** with the sponsored party?
    Sponsorship as a form of co-operations implies the necessity to negotiate and
    interact with ones partner as direct as possible in order to avoid long communica-
    tion channels, misunderstandings and phases of silence. One could say, the less

parties there are involved, the more likely is the co-operation/ sponsorship to become a success.

· Is it the right **music genre**?

The image dimensions of specific music genres differ enormously. A company should first select a small number of music genres with suitable images to its own and then take a deeper look on artists, organisations, etc. from the respective genres.

· Does the sponsored party address the right **target group**?

The sponsored party should be able to provide specific target group information (not only descriptive, but also in shares regarding: sex, age, lifestyle, interests etc.). The structure of the target group should be consistent with the one of the company/brand or product.

· Does the **image of the sponsored party** provide a good fit?

A premium brand needs a top-level partner, a young and dynamic company a similar natured partner in turn and so forth. If a company/brand wants to establish a new image, it has to search for a sponsored party that corresponds to the aspired image and performance, not to the present one. An image analysis is inevitable and can easily be found out by questioning the audience of the sponsored party. A sponsorship is less promising, if it is based on arguments like "We can sell our products on-side at this event, which is enough." or "We sponsor this artist, because we know his management".

· Is the sponsored party **linked with the respective region**?

Companies, which want to advertise on a regional level, need to look for a partner that is known and popular within the region. By supporting local acts, sponsors can win over the "public heart". By supporting national or international acts, the general public involvement might not be as high.

· Is **exclusiveness** warranted?

If companies from other sectors also sponsor the artist, event etc., it usually rather has positive effects on the own sponsorship. But sponsors always need to determine by contract that the sponsored party is not allowed to co-operate with its direct competitors during the contract period of the sponsorship.

· Is there a chance for **regular meetings**?

The sponsor can only react flexible on opportunities and threats in line with the sponsorships, if the sponsored party informs him on a regular basis. Meetings in person always need to be preferred to reports in written form. Moreover, a sponsor can always play a part in the organisation of these meetings.

· Is there an adequate ratio of **giving and taking**?

Although sponsorships underlie the idea of support, a sponsor always needs to consider one question: How much do we get for our money? Sponsored parties mostly offer various and eclectic forms of presentation to the sponsor, which are also relatively low priced compared to classical communication. But as aforementioned, it is not the biggest, but the best appearance that counts. A company needs to filter out the most suitable measures for itself and should not have short-term economic objectives in mind when choosing between them. It rather needs to focus on long-term image effects, in order to increase the impact of the sponsorship with its duration.

· Is the sponsored party able to **demonstrate the advertising effect**?

Due to the higher professionalization of sports sponsorships compared to cultural, i.e. music sponsorships, there are only few managements, organisations etc. that are able to prove the advertising effect that a sponsorship might have. However, when choosing a sponsorship, a company should always try to get as much information possible about outcomes of earlier sponsorships of the potential partner, in order to forecast its very own potential outcomes of the sponsorship.

·   Does the engagement **meet with response from the media**?
Sponsorships do not only take effect on the target group once, but at least twice. It is the music event or other sponsoring measure where the target group has its first contact with the sponsorship. And then it's the media that multiplies the contact rate, by mentioning the sponsor in their news coverage. For this reason, the sponsor should always ask for the sponsored party's press contacts as well as for its press kit of the last months. Moreover, the contractual agreement should include joint press conferences.

Step 3: Developing effective sponsoring measures

·   What kind of **logo integration** and **advertising** is possible (e.g. in printed matters)?

·   Is a presentation at **eye-catching** points possible (e.g. on stage, banner)?

·   Is an **acoustic** presentation possible (e.g. radio advertising, advertising trailers)?

·   Does the target group get the chance to **experience the service or product** respectively read up on it (e.g. product demonstrations, sales at reduced prices, trials, creative and innovative handouts)?

·   Does the own appearance **detract from the actual experience** (e.g. too big or too loud presentation, pure sales motive)?

·   Is there an appropriate and eloquent representative of the sponsoring party present at **press conferences** of the sponsored party?

·   What kind of information material and incentives are provided for the **media** (e.g. product trials)?

·   Does the sponsored party show **outside of its own activities** (e.g. autograph sessions, corporate events)?

· Is it possible to **co-operate with other sponsors** with the objective of addressing the target group (e.g. organise sponsor days, joint events)?

· Does the sponsored party allow **hospitality measures** (e.g. free tickets, VIP lounge, meet and greet)

· Is it meaningful to invite **important clients**, opinion leaders, etc.?

· How can the sponsorship be **incorporated** with other marketing/communication measures (e.g. sales promotion, classical advertisements, public relations)

5. Conclusion

The analysis of the music industry along Porter's five forces has shown that the music business is experiencing a shift in its sources of income: money is no longer made in the studio but instead onstage. For the record labels this means that they increasingly have to start functioning as service providers: besides marketing artists and products they also have the important task of promoting concerts. At the same time, production and distribution of recorded music are becoming less profitable. Meanwhile, players experienced in promoting concerts like Live Nation start to serve as record labels, manager and promoter at the same time. They are therewith able to offer 360 degree deals to artists. Consequently, and thanks to music digitalisation and the Internet, the traditional value chain of the music industry has changed into a complex value creation network: The music industry 2.0.

For potential sponsors, this development opens room for the creation of new business models and for setting up new alliances. Whether it is record companies that are distributing music online via social networking sites, flat-rate music offerings for mobile phones or concert promoters collaborating with the hospitality industry – the music industry is ready and willing to co-operate on a new level, and to integrate sponsoring parties wherever they can. Thus, the music market today provides many new opportunities for the participation and integration of sponsors.

Especially the sponsorship of artists and groups has become more attractive, due to the decreased number of parties involved in the process. For this reason, direct co-operations with top-level artists are now possible for the first time. Additionally, the shift in profitable business areas makes extended, pricey marketing measures inevitable for musicians, which favours the prospect of good deals for the sponsor. The weakened position of record labels empowers sponsors regarding the negotiation of deals and the development of new, joint business plans. And last but not least, communication instruments for music sponsorships, especially online platforms, have developed enormously during the last couple of years so that sponsors now have the opportunity to realise successful music sponsorships with 360 degree activation throughout all marketing channels.

Still, music sponsorship poses the threat of no – or wrong – perception by the target group leading to lasting damages to the image of both parties. The findings of this thesis disclose that companies can prevent these threats with a strategic approach and planning of the sponsorship in line with all other communication and marketing activities. The preparation for sponsorship in general, the right choice of the sponsored party from the music industry and the planning and development of an unique and eclectic set of sponsoring measures are key factors for successful music sponsorships. When taking these points into consideration in times of communication overload within society, music – and therewith music sponsorship – today offer a unique and emotional value added to target groups, better than any other marketing measure ever could.

Bibliography

Books

Bruhn, M., *Planung des Sponsoring*: in Hermans, A.: *Sport- und Kultursponsorsing*, p.15-28, Munich, 1989

Bruhn, M., *Sponsoring. Unternehmen als Mäzene und Sponsoren*, 2nd Edition, Frankfurt am Main, 1991

Bruhn, M., *Integrierte Unternehmens- und Markenkommunikation. Strategische Planung und operative Umsetzung*, 3rd Edition, Stuttgart, 2003

Eggebrecht, H. H., *Musik in unserem Leben* in: Redaktion für Musik des Bibliographischen Instituts, *Meyers kleines Lexikon Musik*, S. 5-11, 1986

Engh, M., *Popstars als Marke*, Gabler/Deutscher Universitätsverlag, 2006

Emes, J., *Unternehmensgewinn in der Musikindustrie: Wertschöpfungspotentiale und Veränderungen in der Branchenstruktur durch die Digitalisierung*, Würzburg, Deutscher Universitätsverlag/GWV Fachverlage GmbH, 2004

Hanrieder, M., *Sport- und Kultursponsoring*, München, Vahlen, 1989

Hermanns, A., *Sponsoring – Grundlagen, Wirkungen, Management, Markenführung*, 3rd Edition, Munich, 2008

Kohlenberg, M., *Musiksponsoring: Grundlagen – Strategien – Beispiele*, Wiesbaden, Deutscher Universitätsverlag, 1994

Nieschlag, R., Dicht, E., Hörschgen, H., *Marketing*, 16th Edition, 1991

Porter, M. E., *Michael E. Porter on Competition and Strategy*, Boston, Harvard Business Press, 1991

Porter, M. E., *Competitive Strategy: Techniques for Analyzing Industries and Competitors*, Free Press, 1998

Ringe, C., *Popstars für Marken*, in: Bronner, K. / Hirt, R., *Audio-Branding: Entwicklung, Anwendung, Wirkung akustischer Identitäten in Werbung, Medien und Gesellschaft*. p. 172-184, München, 2007

Ringe, C., *Pop-Sponsoring und der Traum von der Freiheit. Wie man Popstars glaubhaft sponsert* in: Strahlendorf, P., *Jahrbuch Sponsoring 2008*, p. 164-169, Hamburg, 2008

Spiesecke, H., *IFPI Yearbook 2005*, Musikmarkt, Berlin, 2005

Wirt, B. W., *Integriertes Marken- und Kundenwertmanagement – Strategien, Konzepte und Best Practices*, Gabler, Betriebswirt.-Verlag, 2004

Websites

Definition Sponsorship (IEG Lexicon and Glossary – Free registration to website required)
http://www.sponsorship.com/Resources/IEG-Lexicon-and-Glossary.aspx (2008)

Volkswagen Sound Foundation microsite
http://www.soundfoundation.de (2008)

Usage term Music Industry
http://en.wikipedia.org/wiki/Music_industry (May 2008)

Die Musikindustrie 1.0 ist tot
http://www.boerse-express.com/pages/638529 (28th January 2008)

David Byrne and Thom Yorke on the Real Value of Music
http://www.wired.com/entertainment/music/magazine/16-01/ff_yorke?currentPage=all
(18th December 2007)

Absolut Kravitz microsite www.absolutkravitz.com (2008)

Music Is Driving Growth In Digital Commerce (John Kennedy, CEO and Chairman
IFPI, Speech at ETNO (European Telecommunications Network Operators'
Association Conference)
http://www.ifpi.org/content/section_views/view014.html (3rd March 2005)

Christoph Dallach *Win-Win-Situation*
http://www.spiegel.de/kultur/kulturspiegel/0,1518,502216,00.html (28th July 2007)

*Mit dem Bit Music Contest in die erste Liga des Musikbiz! Nachwuchswettbewerb
bietet Talenten Chance durch nachhaltige Förderung* (Bitburger Press Release)
http://www.presseportal.de/pm/43064/1104800/bitburger/ (18th June 2008)

Dr Pepper Band in Bubble microsite http://www.drpepperbubble.com/ (2008)

iTunes Store Tops Over Five Billion Songs Sold (Apple Press Release)
http://www.apple.com/pr/library/2008/06/19itunes.html (19th June 2008).

Jay-Z to sign deal with Live Nation
http://music.guardian.co.uk/news/story/0,,2270696,00.html (April 3rd 2008).

Studies

German Survey on Sponsoring 2006

IEG Sponsorship Report 2007

IFPI Digital Music Report 2008

Jahrbuch Sponsoring 2008

Spectrum Report 2006

Sponsor Visions 2007

Sponsoring Trends 2006

MARKETING UND KOOPERATIONEN
Herausgegeben von Noshokaty, Döring & Thun, Berlin

Band 1
Angela Hund-Göschel
Music Sponsorship at a Turning Point
Lohmar – Köln 2009 ♦ 84 S. ♦ € 37,- (D) ♦ ISBN 978-3-89936-826-0

JOSEF EUL VERLAG